COALS TO CALCUTTA

COALS TO CALCUTTA

the true story of the daughter of a preacher man

MARGO RUTTER

Copyright © 2010 Margo Rutter

The moral right of the author has been asserted.

Apart from any fair dealing for the purposes of research or private study, or criticism or review, as permitted under the Copyright, Designs and Patents Act 1988, this publication may only be reproduced, stored or transmitted, in any form or by any means, with the prior permission in writing of the publishers, or in the case of reprographic reproduction in accordance with the terms of licences issued by the Copyright Licensing Agency. Enquiries concerning reproduction outside those terms should be sent to the publishers.

Matador
5 Weir Road
Kibworth Beauchamp
Leicester LE8 0LQ, UK
Tel: (+44) 116 279 2299
Fax: (+44) 116 279 2277
Email: books@troubador.co.uk
Web: www.troubador.co.uk/matador

ISBN 978-1848762-473

British Library Cataloguing in Publication Data.
A catalogue record for this book is available from the British Library.

Typeset in 11.5pt Sabon MT by Troubador Publishing Ltd, Leicester, UK

Matador is an imprint of Troubador Publishing Ltd

Printed in Great Britain by the MPG Books Group, Bodmin and King's Lynn

*For Ashley and Cara,
the delights of my life and the joys of my heart*

CONTENTS

Foreword ix
Acknowledgements xiii

Elephants Make Me Cry	1
Little Jimmy	5
On The Rocks	21
Pit to Pulpit	35
Cold Tea and a Railway Bench	42
Just a Little Sign	52
In Humble Service	58
Tears and Pain	68
End of an Era	88
Daughter of a Preacher Man	105
Joy	117
The Pain of Loss	125
A Silent Whisper	136
Southall	153
Divine Respect	163
A Fretful Flight	178
Kolkata Streets	189
Blow Horn Please!	202
Peaceful Contentment	211

FOREWORD
Rev Dr Inderjit S. Bhogal OBE

Margo writes in an honest and engaging way. This book is written in the style of a novel and is easy to read and follow. The writer is on a journey of discovery and the reader becomes her companion, interested to find out what happened next. Each page uncovers the next stage. Along the journey the reader will experience the writers' emotions…anger, delight, confusion, guilt, relief… and wrestle with her questions.

Margo's abiding inspiration is her dad Jim. She tells his story, his roots and routes, his call to Calcutta. Within the context of this story we learn about the rest of the family and Margo's own story as "the daughter of a Preacher man".

As Margo writes, she finds herself on a road of her shifting identity, self starvation and self discovery.

Margo's search for her dad's story takes her to Blackhall, Bradford, Calcutta and Southall. She writes well about his struggles in education, beginnings in hairdressing, work in coal mining, the centering of early life around the local Methodist Chapel, his commitment to preaching the Gospel of Christ, his "pull" towards Methodist Ministry, training for Ministry, and offering to go as a missionary to India, and then a return to English cities with Asian populations.

Jim had never seen an Asian person, never heard of curry, but he undertook training and orientation at Selly Oak College, and learned to speak Hindi.

He and his beloved Irene, travelled to India and arrived in the heart of Kolkata (Calcutta, as it was known then).

Suddenly he was confronted with reality that is India, a crucible of the many religions and the many poor, and, of course, in Calcutta there was Mother Teresa too. This was the context in which Jim's theology was developed in ways that Margo sees as being "in tune" with the teachings and practice of Jesus Christ: compassion for people in need and respect for people of different faiths.

As Jim's work and preaching began to take shape there were issues that were starting to emerge, not least around health and education, for the rest of the family. Jim's own health was detrimentally affected. Irene became seriously ill.

Jim was left with no option but to bring the family back to England, and for the first time Margo became aware of people with white skin.

The family come to live in Bradford and then Southall. The many people of Asian backgrounds here are a plus for Margo. But as she grows she also begins to sense the loss of her dad to the Church. She witnesses people speaking quite rudely to her father in Church. She discovers racism. She is diagnosed with School phobia. She screams out that her Church dominated upbringing has "screwed me up".

In the midst of all this is a blissful and unforgettable day with her dad in a local Park.

Margo writes sensitively and honestly about life in a Manse, a house that is so often filled with stories of Church and people in Church.

Margo's own spirituality emerges out of all her life experiences including loss and change, poverty and suffering, and the recognition that Christianity is practised in a world of many religions. The big question "Is Jesus the only way to God?" is not avoided. She writes about the dangers of people living in their own cages of tradition, and the need to challenge them to stretch their boundaries, and so be enriched. Caring for Irene in her final illness raises questions about God and Pastoral Care, and leaves Margo searching for healing herself.

God became real to Jim in the darkness of coal mine pits and the hustle and bustle of life in Calcutta. Margo "the loner" finally discovers the reality of God beside the Sea, and speaks of "the God of the Beach". She returns to India, treads on familiar ground again, and finds healing in Kolkata.

I knew Jim well and had enormous respect for him. We first met when he invited me to Southall. This was my first visit to this bit of Panjab in London. Jim introduced me to many of his Sikh friends with a sense of great pride. He took me to a room in King's Hall Methodist Church which had become a centre for Sikh – Christian dialogue. I was so impressed. He believed it was part of his practise as a follower of Jesus Christ to engage in honest, open dialogue with people of other faiths, and to foster good relationships of mutual respect and trust. Irene too found great delight in this ministry that Jim was engaged in.

Both Jim and Irene treated me with respect, and seemed to find encouragement through my support. We became friends for life.

I only met Margo after Jim and Irene had died, and encouraged her to write this book. I particularly felt that Jim's story needed to be told. I am honoured to write these opening words.

What it is to be a follower of Christ in a world of many religions and deep poverty remains a challenge. Religion and Faith are hot topics of discussion today. Religious and secular writers are engaged in the debate. Margo's book provides a helpful contribution. There is illumination here and the difficult questions are not avoided.

Inderjit Bhogal
Former President of the Methodist Church
August 2009

ACKNOWLEDGEMENTS

Occasionally chance meetings alter the course of our comfortably organised lives. Bob Shipman is a well travelled man who embraces any opportunity to explore new horizons. When I bumped into him one sunny afternoon his infectious enthusiasm challenged me. And so it is to you Bob, that I say thank you, for it was your advice and encouragement that fuelled me with the courage to go in search of that great city of joy. It was there that I had the great pleasure of being introduced to Mala and Babil, thank you to you also.

Many thanks go to you Inderjit Bhogal, for your encouragement, support and valued contribution towards this book.

I thank Harry Archbold, and all the members of the Blackhalls Local History Group for their fascinating and informative publications which proved to be an invaluable source for my research.

My heartfelt gratitude goes to many people for their support. Gordon Forrest, whose constructive criticism, proof reading and endless encouragements have been much appreciated. My cousin Keith Hewson, for sharing your vast knowledge of family history with me and for leading me through long grassed muddy fields in search of foundational proof. Many thanks also to Joan and Ernest Bradley, Silvia and Billy Lister, Jean and Jim Pritchard and my very dear Auntie Evelyn Robinson. The support of all my friends has been overwhelming and has touched me deeply, thank you.

I would like to take this opportunity to pay my deep respects to the late Edwin Bradley and his wife Winny. The bond of love and friendship between them and Jimmy and Irene was strong indeed.

It is with much love that I acknowledge my big brother Steve Parkinson, whom I look up to now even more than I did as a child. Your honour, sincerity, integrity and compassion make me deeply proud to be your sister.

Finally, Garry, Ashley and Cara, thank you from the bottom of my heart for your love and support. I'm sure, during the writing of this book, that there were times when you could have, quite cheerfully, locked me in the study and thrown away the key but instead you encouraged, loved and hugged me. I love you more than I can express and am so very thankful for the loving family life that we share.

ELEPHANTS MAKE ME CRY

'*I am the resurrection and the life, says the Lord...*' No, No, No, I wanted to shout, something's wrong, it's the voice, the wrong voice, it's not his voice. '*He who believes in me, though he die, yet shall he live...*' I felt the blood rush to my ears and my knees began to tremble. I put my fingers to my temples and pressed them firmly but still the voice continued, '*and whoever lives and believes in me shall not die eternally*'. The minister walked soberly up the aisle dressed in a long black cassock. He was followed by six, black suited, pall bearers carrying the oak coffin, except I knew that the oak was only a veneer to grace the pale plywood beneath. The minister walked in front of us in the front row of the crematorium and smiled gently, with sincere compassion in his eyes. He took his place behind the lectern to our right, the pall bearers laid the coffin, adorned with the floral arrangements we'd lovingly chosen, in the centre. The minister began to speak again and the organ stirred into life with the strains of a hymn. I tried to sing the words written on the page of my hymnbook but tears blurred my vision and a lump constricted my throat, all that came out was a croak.

    The front wall of the little chapel, behind the coffin, was made of glass. It was a clear, crisp autumnal day and the sun shone through the glass and danced its reflections off the coffin's brass handles and hinges. Outside the last of the summer's leaves, transformed into coppery hues, clung to the branches of their trees, just as I tried to cling onto my composure.

Surely this is all a mistake. Surely Dad will appear. Any moment now he will walk up the aisle and cross in front of us wearing his long black cassock and gown with his white dog collar inserted into the stand-up collar of his shirt. As it's a funeral he'll have his special narrow, silky stole draped around the back of his neck to hang respectfully down the front of his gown. He'll walk along the row with his huge grin lighting up his face. He'll wink at me and my brother, his son and daughter-in-law and his grandchildren, then he'll give Mum his special smile, the one that's just for her, the smile that says 'my lovely Irene'. Then he'll take his place beside the minister at the lectern, they'll smile in amicable acknowledgement, and his rich, deep voice will resound around the room and bounce off the glass wall and all will be well again.

But no, Dad, my Dad, is in that coffin. I know this to be true because I was there by his side when he drew his last breath. As if to confirm that his body breathed no more I went to the chapel of rest with my brother. There I saw his lifeless state, the shell of his body dressed in his best black suit and clerical shirt. That's when I saw the plywood beneath the oak veneer. My brother examined the craftsmanship of the coffin and tapped it. He said, 'Mmm, it's not bad Dad, they've done a good job for you, but you would have made it better yourself'.

*

Dad died a few years ago; I had just reached the age of forty.

His final few weeks of life were filled with agonising pain; his body was riddled with cancer; it was nasty. And yet, there was something going on inside that man that was a marvel to encounter. The night before his death I sat beside his bed that was set up in the lounge of my parents' home, and held his hand as I sang to him. He was being fed a high dose of morphine through a clear plastic tube and past the stage of being able to talk. But as I made my way through his hymn book, choosing hymns I'd heard him sing a thousand times and more, he occasionally squeezed my fingers and I knew that he was aware. In those final hours of his life on this earth an ocean's depth of strength and pure joy emanated from him. In death, as in life he was content. There were no regrets for his chosen way of life, through thick and thin he had always maintained that he would do it all over again. In his youth he made a commitment to love and serve his God to the end of his days. He did not betray that commitment.

When our Mum died, just a few short years after Dad, having suffered a grotesque, hospital-induced superbug, my brother and I looked at each other in recognition of our newly orphaned state. Mum, like Dad, left this earth with her faith in God fully intact. But unlike Dad, she did not leave convincing me that she was filled with peace and serenity. That she loved and praised God to the end I am positive. That God was there, cradling her in His arms, I was just not sure.

To say that I mourn the death of my parents is an understatement but I have memories and joys in abundance. Their peculiarities were many and fill me with laughter. Mum's love of elephants fills my loft with carved wooden elephants, soapstone elephants and pictures of elephants. My study is home to families of cuddly elephants, rings of elephants to hold incense sticks and pen pot holders with long trunks and I wonder when I will at last be able to, really, smile at them without a tear coming into my eye.

But the big question that fills my being, now that my parents are gone is God, the God who directed their joint journey through life. I have always assumed a belief in their God and have ambled through life blinkered and accepting. In my naivety and trusting assurance that my parents were right I realise, with a shock, that I have never deeply questioned my own personal beliefs. The time has come for me to face the challenge.

Another aspect of being born the daughter of a preacher man is roots. The Church had us moving around periodically from district to district so I don't really know where I am from or where I belong. These questions have become important to me so I am going on a journey of discovery. My starting point is my Dad's beginning, my parent's roots.

LITTLE JIMMY

Jimmy Parkinson was born on the third day of November 1925 in Trimdon Grange, a village perhaps better associated with a well-known figure by the name of Anthony Charles Linton Blair than a small boy with prominent front teeth.

My journey begins as I leave home, a little apprehensively, waving goodbye to my two young adult children and my husband, Rock. Please be assured that this is not his real name but it does suit his character and self image. I'm heading for the North East of England and the county of Durham from a small town in Worcestershire. A long drive lay ahead of me and for the first hour I frowned a lot as I pictured many scary scenarios of things that could go wrong as I travelled alone. My tyres could burst, the windscreen could crack, the hotel may have forgotten about my booking, or a wild ferocious tiger on the loose could leap through my open window at any second. I closed the window a few inches, turned up the music and sang along heartily with Nelly Furtado, *'I'm like a bird, I'll only fly away, I don't know where my home is, I don't know where my soul is'*.

As I settled into the drive I thought about my Dad, Jim. He was an unpretentious man and often described as a little man with a big smile. He had a highly infectious laugh that rippled through a crowd like a pebble dropped into a pond. His eyes held a twinkle of mischief and a depth of earnest compassion. He had a personable face and a charismatic personality. His poverty-stricken up-bringing in the world of mining kept his feet on the ground and taught him to remain true to his values. He was, in my opinion, a man of deep integrity.

Waste of any description was abhorrent to him. Waste of money, waste of food and water, waste of life. He had a keen mind and loved to work out how things were made and put together so that he could rebuild and repair anything broken. My very first car, when I was twenty one, was a maroon coloured *Renault 5* and I was fiercely proud of it and the new independence it afforded me. The car's shell was in good shape but the engine ran into a few problems. Jim stuck his head under the bonnet and did a bit of tinkering before declaring that he would look around the scrap yards for a replacement engine. Until he found the right one, at a price he approved of, he informed me that I would have to keep an eye on the idling jet.

'The what?' I asked. He directed my attention to a little valve attached to a hose feeding petrol from the tank into the engine.

'Now you see this valve here?' he said as he pointed to a gold but greasy looking part about three quarters of an inch long.

'Yes', I replied.

'Well now, you remove it like this', there followed a demonstration, 'and then you take one of these bristles, I've put a few in an envelope for you in the glove compartment'.

'Thank you', I acknowledged.

'Now because the petrol tank has obviously been running on low far too often it's dredged up all the sludge at the bottom and is blocking the flow through the idling jet'.

'Well I never', I responded as he handed me a clean bristle from Mum's garden broom.

'Hold the valve up to the light and look through the hole in the middle'.

'I can't see a hole', I said.

'That's because it's blocked but if you push the bristle through it you'll clear the blockage'.

'Ah yes', I agreed. 'So how often do I have to do this?' I asked nervously.

'Every time the engine cuts out. You'll have to use foot control on the accelerator to keep the petrol flowing when you stop at junctions and roundabouts but if it does cut out just do this'.

A five mile journey could see my bottom sticking out from beneath the bonnet as many as six times, while curious and furious drivers tooted their horns impatiently behind me. But true to his word, Jim devised a ramp and a pulley wheel to hang from the ceiling of his garage and fitted a newly conditioned engine that ran like clockwork for many years.

Washing machines and cookers all got the Jimmy treatment too as he fitted drums and hoses rescued from scrap heaps. His garage was a veritable treasure chest of nuts, bolts, screws and hinges; he even had a small wooden box filled with magnifying glasses and minute brushes for cleaning the workings of wrist watches and clocks. He'd turn his hand to anything. When computers flooded the market, he didn't simply buy a package all neatly sold in a box, but scoured 'for sale' notices and bought each item second-hand, then put them together himself. Irene sucked dust and fluff from every house she lived in, with the same old Hoover they'd received as a wedding present.

Modern dentistry was a marvel to him. Thankfully he did refrain from having a go himself but he was so impressed with the speed at which the drill emptied a rotten tooth that he insisted, 'You don't need an injection in your gum when you have a filling pet, the drills work so quickly that the discomfort is hardly noticeable and you won't have to put up with that awful numbness afterwards'. Consequently I spent many painful moments in the dentist's chair with my fingers gripped tightly around the arms as my feet twitched involuntarily.

Jim inherited his father's tools of trade. Long scissors, short scissors for fine trimming, a pair of thinning scissors and manually operated shears were all lovingly preserved and kept wrapped in a white cotton sheet in his desk drawer. Every month I sat on his desk and he draped the sheet around my shoulders and had me close my eyes while he snipped my fringe. The thinning scissors were not easy to sharpen and felt as though they were pulling my hair out by the roots. I'm so thankful that I didn't have to suffer the shears like my brother Timu did. My first encounter with a hairdressing salon happened when I was fourteen, and was a complete revelation to me.

He insisted that Timu and I learn basic do-it-yourself skills as soon as he thought we were up to it. He had us decorating rooms, lying on our backs staring up at 'U' bends, hanging shelves from walls and making bookcases. Timu is now an extremely gifted woodworker in his spare time and I've been quite handy with a kango hammer in mine.

Four hours after leaving home I arrived in Hartlepool unharmed, with my car intact and minus a tiger and very relieved to note that the hotel had reserved a room for me. It took me a while to get to sleep that first night. Every sound and snore made me jump and every few minutes I checked that my room was locked securely. After a comforting conversation with Rock on my mobile phone I settled down. I was excited about this trip and couldn't wait to visit the places of Jimmy and Irene's youth.

I awoke to a harsh, shrill sound echoing around the room and hurting my ears. 'FIRE, FIRE, FIRE!' I yelled aloud in my semi-conscious state; the clock said it was six fifteen in the morning. I leapt out of bed and ran around in panic stricken little circles. Scrambling into clothes I made for the door on limbs that felt detached from the rest of my body. I joined the stampede of other bemused guests and was ushered outside onto the harbour of Hartlepool's marina. It was fiercely cold and I felt my lips turn blue and watched my fingers turn white. I suddenly wondered why I had chosen to come here in January as I slipped on the frost covered ground. Icy winds whipped through the car park as the frost draped boats bobbed energetically on the water. Of all the many scary scenarios I had imagined, this had not been one.

Fire engines appeared with sirens blaring as hotel staff checked guests, in various states of dress, off their lists. Pyjamas could be seen under overcoats and men in billowing shirt sleeves stood close to one another as they each spoke loudly into mobile phones. A young woman shivered from head to toe in her fluffy lavender dressing gown and then one poor man came running out with wet hair and a standard white towel wrapped around his cuddly waist. I feared for the man in the strength of the violently strong wind, and hoped fervently that it didn't catch a corner of the towel and completely expose him to the elements. It would have brought a bit of excitement to the trauma though.

After about forty-five minutes of numbingly cold

wonderings regarding the future of the building containing all our belongings we got the all clear. By which time the half-naked gentleman had been provided with a blanket but I'd noticed he was having difficulty in holding both that and the towel in place. Many exhaled sighs of huge relief and ran for cover and warmth. Our friend, whose sandy-coloured hair had dried to a most lively style, walked back into the hotel with an expression of quiet consternation on his face. There had, apparently, been no fire at all just a little problem of an electrical nature. So that was alright then. Once I'd thawed out I set off to explore my surroundings.

Jimmy only spent the first months of his life in Trimdon Grange from where his father ran his business. When the miner's strike of 1926 shook the Durham coalfields and brought the mines and the business to a standstill the family had to relocate and moved to Cold Hesleden. Both Jimmy's mother and father had lived in and around the small village, known locally as the Waterworks, for a large part of their lives. Cold Hesleden, originally an agricultural community, assumed the role of a mining community as the extensive coalmine of close-by Murton over-spilled its workers into it. Bemused ploughmen, inhaling the rich aroma of newly turned earth and fresh air as they guided their horse-drawn ploughs in steady rhythm across beloved land, shuddered as they watched soot-blackened men return to their homes after a day spent toiling below ground.

Mining went a long way back in Jimmy's family history. All the Parkinson men on his father's side, and there were many, for those miners were a virile lot, had submitted themselves into the mines around the county of Durham. Most had completed their education and begun work at the age of eight to twelve years old. His maternal grandfather had come to Murton colliery from the Welsh Valleys.

John Evans's father, Solomon, had gone to work as normal in the pit of Hafod Colliery, but as he was hewing the coal with his pick the prop holding up the roof of the seam gave way. As he lay on his back to reach the tightly packed coal, the weight of the rock above his body loosened and, with a mighty thunder it tumbled like a cascading avalanche and crushed the very last breath of life out of him. John reeled from the shock of his father's cruel death and in his sorrow took it upon himself to leave the community in which he'd been raised. Having heard a rumour on the grapevine that pit work was plentiful and rates of pay good he headed off, at the age of twenty four, for pastures new. He aimed for the distant shores of England's North East coastline where he believed he'd be able to make enough money to live on plus an amount to send home to his widowed mother.

My romantic side likes to picture the scene of a band of rugged Welsh men standing on the top of picnic mountain in Rhosllanerchrugog, moor of the heathery glade, singing in rich harmony a powerful farewell as they waved him goodbye: *'Far away a voice is calling, bells of memory do shine, come home again, come home again they called through the oceans of time. We'll keep a welcome in the hillside, we'll keep a welcome in the vales, this land you knew will still be singing when you come home again to Wales'*. I see a young John Evans wiping the tears from his eyes with his jacket sleeve as he set off on foot. He walked, yes walked from Wales to Durham with only a little loose change in his pocket. He found work here and there along the way and slept rough when he couldn't afford shelter.

John never did return home to Wales to sing in baritone. Within a short time he met a miner's daughter, originally from Carlisle, and fell in love. Libby already had a ten-year-old daughter by a man who apparently didn't know his own name, or so the birth certificate stated. John willingly accepted the little girl as his own and he and Libby married and began to extend their family, although it appears that their first-born son developed very quickly in the womb as he arrived in the world just five weeks after the wedding. They continued to produce another five children, one of whom was Elizabeth, a little girl with big, beautiful brown eyes.

Elizabeth, or Lizzie as she became affectionately known, grew up in the vicinity of Murton and Cold Hesleden. She became adept in the art of dress-making and worked up a little business that she ran from her parents' home. She helped her mother to run the house and took care of her two younger cousins for her widowed uncle who had come to live with them from Wales. Uncle Evan Evans had only one and a half legs due to an accident in the Welsh mines. His left leg stopped at the knee where it engaged with a specially designed wooden lower leg. He had a strange habit of whittling his false leg with a small, sharp knife as he whistled merry tunes. He got a bit carried away at times and found he'd carved a perfect ball at the foot and became prone to walking around in circles.

When Lizzie Evans embarked upon a relationship of a romantic nature with James Parkinson, she thought that if they were to marry, how wonderful it would be not to have to deal with his filthy pit clothes at the end of each day. Jim, as every one called him, was not a miner. His father had worked in the pit from the age of twelve and had watched helplessly as his four eldest sons followed him. He encouraged his two youngest boys to break the mould and set them up with jobs at the pumping station in the village. As soon as they each reached the age of sixteen he sent them off to serve apprenticeships in hairdressing in Newcastle and Gateshead.

Lizzie and Jim did marry, around the time in modern history that ladies' skirts were shortened to just above the ankle. They were harshly separated for their first few years of wedded bliss by the First World War in which Jim served as a machine-gunner. He was sent to fight in France and Lizzie was left alone and pregnant with their first child. On his return he secured the barber's shop on Trimdon Grange's Front Street and they resumed the pleasant exercise of making babies. Following four little girls, little Jimmy arrived into the world.

From Hartlepool I set off along the A19 towards Murton in eager anticipation of a gentle stroll around Cold Hesleden. The signpost announced my arrival just off the roundabout, so with great joy and eyes wide I drove ahead. I could find no evidence of a village anywhere. I saw one or two detached houses, a garden centre and a huge, impressive gothic style building that was cordoned off. I pulled into the opening of the building and glowered at the notice informing me, in no uncertain terms, to keep out. With its intricate brickwork around tall, narrow arched windows it made an imposing sight. This had to be the old pumping station. A further notice confirmed my suspicions but told me that it had now been sold to a company with plans to transform it into a night-time venue and restaurant. I knew that little Jimmy had lived opposite the waterworks and that the place had frightened the wits out of him for he had been convinced that it was full of ghosts.

With a sinking heart I looked across the road and saw an industrial estate. One of the detached houses I'd seen earlier had a distinct resemblance to an old style chapel but I saw no sign of a village school. This was not boding well. I decided to drive into Murton to see if I could find a library that could explain the mysterious disappearance of Cold Hesleden. At the library I learned that it had been demolished sometime around the late 1960s to early 70s.

Walking through Murton's pedestrian shopping street revived my saddened heart as I noticed a bingo hall. I've never played the game in my life but the words 'Empire' stood out on the building's frontage in large blue letters. When Jim and Lizzie left Trimdon Grange with the closure of the pit, Jim leased a plot attached to the Empire cinema building in Murton. This was it, the address was correct. On rare occasions, when money permitted the luxury, little Jimmy had come to this cinema with his Dad to watch Charlie Chaplin's silent movies or his favourite films of cowboys and Indians.

As luck, chance, or fate would have it an elderly lady asked me why I was taking a photograph of the old cinema. I explained what I was doing and her eyes lit up at the mention of Cold Hesleden. 'I have a picture of the village as it used to be, my mother used to live there, come with me and I'll give it to you', she ordered. I did question myself as to whether or not I should follow her but my curiosity got the better of me. The eccentric lady with her shock of bold, untamed grey hair, wearing scarlet lipstick but not enough fixative on her false teeth, led me to her house and produced a black and white aerial photograph of the entire village. I was overjoyed and offered profuse thanks to which she replied, 'It's my pleasure, didn't know what to do with it anyway', as she shut her front door in my face.

Back at the industrial estate I was able to make out the shape and boundary of the village. It had been made up of five blocks of terraced houses, each with its own allotment and outside privy. The only school stood on the outskirts and it looks as though the now converted house was indeed the chapel. The pumping station, in the photo, had a tower that was now gone, but I had also learned from my eccentric friend that German aircraft used it as a bomber's guide to find their way to the shipyards of Middlesborough, Newcastle and Tyneside, which they then bombarded.

I walked around the estate, attracting a few curious looks from van drivers, and managed to locate the whereabouts of little Jimmy's house, number 1 Hesleden Terrace, and felt a sudden surge of elation.

Jimmy looked forward to starting school. Being the youngest child he was bored at home once all his sisters were gone for the day and he wanted to go with them. He soon came to rue the day that he'd wished for. Right from the very beginning Jimmy and school simply did not gel. His days were crammed with confusion, humiliation and pain. He'd sense the approach of the fearsome, unsmiling teacher as she fixed her eyes on him, making her way to his wooden desk with the little hole cut out of its lid for the inkwell. Like an overblown balloon she'd stand over him with her arm raised. He'd brace himself as the ruler hovered above him and grit his teeth as it whistled through the air and came down with uncanny precision upon his tender little knuckles.

He could never understand what it was he did to fuel the wrath of the huge, red-faced teacher who smelt of boiled onions. He'd turn to throw an imploring look at his sister Betty, 'What have I done now?' the look would question. Betty would glare at his hands and he'd follow her eyes and notice that he was fiddling with his pencil. He'd turn back and shrug his shoulders in a helpless gesture as if to say, 'But

I just can't help it', catching, once again, the attention of the big balloon. This time it was the back of his knees that felt the searing pain as Fatty Hattie's big flabby hands struck them hard leaving her bright red handprints on his white skin below his rough woollen shorts. If it wasn't physical pain he endured it was the humiliation of being dragged to the front of the class to be told he was ignorant and stupid in front of all his classmates. Poor little Jimmy could not get the measure of either reading, writing or arithmetic and as that was pretty much what the school day demanded he was fated from the start.

But he was a popular boy and had many friends. He knew everybody in the village and if he slouched his way to school across the allotments, with head hung low as he scraped his feet along the ground, then he made up for it as he ran, jumped and skipped his way back home. Away from school he was happy, enjoying the mischief of games like knocky nine door, where he and his friends would knock on someone's front door and then run like the clappers as they heard footsteps approach. Sometimes they'd tie a piece of string onto the handles of two doors and then knock on both of them. Then as the people inside tried to open them they'd be stuck. Life was one big game of tig, football, marbles and go-carting on home-made carts they put together themselves from orange crates and old pram wheels. Even collecting buckets of water from the communal stand pipe with the top shaped liked a lion's head was fun as water games erupted, often resulting in a clip around the ear from his Mam as he returned home soaking wet with a half-empty bucket.

Weekends were his favourite times, especially in the summer when he'd walk to the beach at Seaham Harbour with his friends and sisters on a Saturday. Then on Sundays he'd go to chapel in the morning with his Mam and sisters all dressed up in their Sunday best and he'd get to walk with his Dad who'd shut the shop for the day of rest. They'd come back after the service and the kitchen would be all warm and smell of roasting beef or lamb. His Dad would take off his jacket and roll up his shirt sleeves and get Jimmy to do the same. 'That's it son', he'd say, 'with sleeves rolled up we're ready for anything'. As his Mam and the girls strained the home-grown vegetables from their pans of steaming hot water his Dad taught him how to carve the meat and divide it among the warm dinner plates. Just as they all sat at the table with knives and forks before them Lizzie would open the oven to reveal golden, crisp, blown-up Yorkshire puddings. Gwennie, the eldest daughter, would put a big hot jug of thick brown gravy in the middle of the table, then they'd all put their hands together and close their eyes as Jim said grace.

Replete after the luxurious treat of Sunday dinner, Jim and Lizzie settled down for an afternoon nap while Jimmy and the girls walked back along to the chapel for Sunday school. This wasn't like weekday school, Jimmy didn't get smacked or whacked on a Sunday. He loved going to learn about the Bible stories and he found he could listen and learn from the kind and patient teachers who took time to explain things to him. He liked to sing songs as well and colour in pictures of the stories they listened to as they were read out aloud.

The very best thing about Sundays was that Jimmy got to spend time with his Dad. His Dad was his real hero, he idolised him in a house full of women. During the week, apart from Wednesday afternoon which was half-day closing for shops, he hardly saw him at all as he was often in bed by the time Jim got home from work. But very occasionally on a Wednesday they'd go to the cinema by his shop together.

Money was really tight in Jimmy's house and it was the same in all his friends' houses. Even though Jim worked many long hours and Lizzie sat up until midnight sewing by lamplight trying to finish off an order for a customer on her Singer machine, which stood next to the big black-leaded fireplace, there was still never any money to spare. But despite their poverty Lizzie did everything she could to ensure that her children always got a halfpenny to spend on a Saturday morning at Forbes's sweet shop in the village. It could take Jimmy almost a whole hour to choose his sweets out of all the bottles and boxes on display. Annie Forbes must have breathed a huge sigh of relief when at last she got to pour the quarter pound of black bullets into a little white paper bag from the metal dish of her weighing scales.

The only time the children had their pocket money withheld was if they hadn't fulfilled their chores during the week. They all had to take a turn at fetching water as there was no running water in the house. The girls helped with cooking, cleaning and washing of clothes and pots. Jimmy dealt mainly with hoying coal with his shovel and bucket from the coal house and making sure there was always a bucket full of ash from the fire next to the netty. The netty, as they called the earth closet, was across the road outside the back of the house by the allotments, housed in a brick midden. It had a wooden door with a metal latch and the brick built closet had a smooth plank of wood laid across it with a hole in the middle. A big nail stuck out of the wall with a loop of string hanging off it holding squares of torn-up newspaper to use as loo roll. Jimmy liked the *Daily Mail* best because the print didn't come off onto his bottom. The ashes were used to pour into the loo after someone had used it, helping to keep down any odours.

Then a man with a horse and cart and a big shovel came along to clean it all out and take it away to dispose of somewhere on the outskirts of the village.

Apart from school Jimmy loved his young life and the friendly village he lived in, where everybody stopped to talk to each other. There was only one thing that scared him apart from flabby hands, rulers and canes. The big old Victorian building on the opposite side of the road to the village frightened the life out of him. It was dark, eerie and shrouded in mystery, set behind large trees. Even by daylight he never walked, always ran looking over his shoulder as he passed it. Strange noises like thuds, groans and howls came from it during the night and its lights flickered dimly from the tall narrow windows. Sometimes Jimmy peeked through the curtains of the bedroom window he shared with his four sisters and saw ghosts and roaming creatures appear round its tower. Their eyes, illuminated in the dark, looked right at him making him shiver and dive into the middle of the bed, startling his sisters and making them scream.

Jim, who'd worked at the waterworks when he was a young boy after he'd left school, had tried to explain to Jimmy that there was nothing to be frightened of inside the building. 'The noises you can hear are the big wheels turning and the pumps pumping the water through all the pipes. There are some beautiful machines in there painted a lovely green with red and gold patterns around them'.

'How come you worked there and not in the pit at Murton Dad?' little Jimmy asked.

'Me Da didn't want me to be a miner son, he said it was a hard, filthy job that played havoc with your bones and he wouldn't want you to do it neither'.

'Well why did you not keep working at the waterworks then?' he persisted.

'I wouldn't have minded that but me Da said I should go with me brother, Tom, and learn how to be a hairdresser, so I did'.

'Do you like being a hairdresser Dad?'

'Not really son, but there's worse things I could do, it's a clean, honest living'.

'Will you teach me to cut hair Dad, so I can come and work with you?'

'Ay son, I will that', said Jim as he ruffled little Jimmy's hair.

'Dad?'

'Yes son?'

'Are there really ghosts in the big tower at the waterworks?'

'No son, they're all in the long tunnels and corridors in the basement'.

ON THE ROCKS

Jimmy's story was beginning to unravel before my eyes as I drove away from Cold Hesleden. On my way to Blackhall, I passed through villages whose names had often rolled off his tongue, like Hawthorn, Easington and Horden. Once there I could almost see the little brown eyed, brown haired nine-year-old boy running towards his friends, playing football with a tin can on the cobbled back street.

'Me Dad's dead', he's shouting, 'me Dad's dead'. It was a moment of excitement, something different had happened and he was at the heart of it. He felt very important as he made his proclamation. All wide eyes were upon him as his friends fired questions of how, why and when. He joined in the game but soon lost interest and ran back home to the flat above his Dad's hairdresser's shop. The bell above the glass door clanged as he pushed it open and again as it closed. He walked across the floor, making footprints in the hair clippings waiting to be swept up by his Dad's busy young assistant, William. He thought about the man with a limp who came once a week to buy the hair so he could stuff mattresses with it. Disappearing through the back door of the shop he ran up the stairs, two at a time and burst into the living room to find his Mam sitting at the table wiping her eyes with a cotton handkerchief. The room was unusually quiet. Jimmy was unaccustomed to such an atmosphere when his four sisters were gathered together. The four girls usually emitted sounds of laughter and joy as they provoked and cajoled each other.

Gwennie, a nurse and the eldest at eighteen comforted her mother with a cup of tea while fourteen-year-old Ella, temporarily released on compassionate grounds from her service at Hardwick Hall, the big manor house, voiced the practical problems facing them all. Eleven-year-old Margaret and ten-year-old Betty fussed over little Jimmy, hugging him tightly. A man with a sombre face, dressed in a black suit with a long tail coat, came through into the room and removed his hat. He had a piece of paper in his hand printed with the name of the grocery shop on Middle Street, *The Co-operative Funeral Services*, it read at the top of the page.

They'd only moved to Blackhall Colliery two years before Jim died. Blackhall was an up and coming mining village with an electrically operated pit that was at peak production and employed almost two and a half thousand men. The village was expanding in a north to south direction along the coast and prospects for local businesses were good. Jim had alternated his working hours between two shops, one at Blackhall where they lived, and one at Horden, the next pit village along the coast. He walked the few miles up and down Horden's steep bank or across the viaduct four times a day to build up business and fit in around the miners' shifts.

Jimmy had hoped, when they left Cold Hesleden, that he might get on better in his new school at Blackhall. Regrettably that was not to be. He seemed to be quite unable to gain favour with any teacher and he managed to get himself on the very wrong side of 'Titchy' Smith in particular. He walked out of the school gates for the very last time with little more education than he'd had on the day he'd first walked in. But he did have a nice collection of stripes on his backside and a great circle of friends.

The jubilation he felt on his very last day, just after he'd turned fourteen, was marred. He walked down to the beach for a few moments of solitude and crossed the blackened sand to sit on a rock at the mouth of a small cave. The sea was relatively calm on that clear fresh day but sometimes it was ferocious with the waves running, rolling and leaping like a lion on the hunt for its prey with its mane tossing wildly in the wind. As he gazed it looked like a giant cauldron of black ink resting on the simmer after its bubbling boil. Jimmy's emotions were like the ever changing sea. It wasn't meant to have been like this. He should be in his Dad's double fronted shop now on Middle Street, sweeping up the hair trimmings with the broom that stood in the corner by the store cupboard. He should be paying close attention to his Dad's skills and learning how to trim hair and lather the chins of pale complexioned miners before deftly taking the sharp blade to remove their stubble.

It had been five years since his Dad, Jim, died at the age of just forty-nine. He'd got a cough that grew worse with each day until he'd started to cough up blood. The weight had dropped off his solid, muscular frame and he began to shiver and convulse with fever. Jimmy remembered the day of the funeral as though it was yesterday. After a service in the Primitive Methodist Chapel they'd all gone to the cemetery and watched the coffin as it was lowered into the deep hole in the ground. 'Ashes to ashes', the minister had said, 'dust to dust'. Then two men had shovelled the soil from the hole back on top of his Dad and they'd had to walk away and leave him there, alone. Lizzie hadn't had enough money to pay for a headstone for the grave so there he lay, unmarked.

They'd stayed on in the flat for another year with William, the assistant, running the business but the rent was high and it became a struggle. A new development at Blackhall Rocks included an estate of council housing on Mickle Hill. Most of the houses were semi-detached and practically built with gardens and the luxury of an indoor bathroom with hot and cold running water. The toilets were outside but attached to the house. Lizzie, in her predicament, was granted one of the new houses on Ocean View but as there were four girls and one boy in the family they were soon moved round the corner to a house with a third bedroom on Tweddle Crescent.

Jimmy picked up a stone from the sand, its rough edges smoothed and worn by the constant ebb and flow of the tide. He leaned to his right and swung his arm out to the side, moving it backwards and forwards until he was satisfied with his angle and rhythm. With his index finger hooked around the smooth, flat stone he brought his arm powerfully around and released it as he swung his body round to the left. One, two, three, four, five, six, seven times it skimmed the top of the water before sinking to the floor of the ocean. He grinned and punched the air with force.

The sand was heavily stained with black tide marks, reminding him of his fate. No amount of crying into his pillow at night had brought his Dad back to him. He couldn't go off somewhere to be trained as a hairdresser, like he'd always wanted, because they needed a main breadwinner to provide for the family. Gwennie was away nursing, both Ella and Margaret worked in service at Hardwick Hall and Betty, the ambitious one, was still at school. She'd passed the entrance examination to Henry Smith's grammar school in Hartlepool and travelled in by bus. Jimmy was due to start work at the pit the next day.

He was small for his age, a good head and shoulders below most of his friends and peers. When he was put to work on the belts at the surface of pit he hit a few problems. Tubs of coal were tipped onto the conveyor belts from the tippling house and men or, as in Jimmy's case, boys, stood at intervals either side of the belt. Their job was to sort out the stones and waste to be discarded. But Jimmy had trouble reaching the belts and spent most of his time jumping up and clinging onto the side to stop himself from being carried along. They were made up of steel strips that overlapped each other, creating a deafening screech, and could be deadly sharp and have a finger off in a moment's daydream. Thankfully he was on datal work which meant that he was paid by the day rather than piece or he may have gone home empty handed. Clearly this was not the right job for a little lad so he was moved onto the tokens in the weigh cabin instead.

The hewers, the men that cut the coal from the face, all had oval shaped metal tokens with their own specific number engraved on them. Each day they collected their tokens and handed one to the banksman before descending in the cage, so that he knew how many men were underground. Once they arrived at the bottom of the pit shaft they gave another token to the deputy overman so that the men underground could be identified in an emergency. When a hewer had cut his coal and filled his tub he'd hang another token onto the side, as would the putter who hauled the tub so that the check-weighman could verify their wages according to the weight of coal cut and hauled. Jimmy's job was to collect all the tokens after they'd been checked and hang them onto the allotted loops.

Bob Bradley was a check-weighman at Blackhall colliery. A fair man employed by both the colliery and the miners themselves as their representative. In the past, before unions and fair play, the miners had been diddled by the collieries' weighmen who had the sneaky habit of under weighing the tubs. Bob checked the weighmen in a safeguard against foul play. He knew Jimmy as he and Bob's eldest son, Edwin, had formed a good friendship in school. Aware that his father was dead Bob took him under his wing and made sure that he had a man he could turn to. At lunchtimes he sent Jimmy to his own house to collect his bait box, knowing that his wife Freda would make a fuss of him while he was there.

As soon as Jimmy reached the age of sixteen he was sent to work below ground. Every morning he'd leave home at five o'clock, while it was still pitch dark in the winter, and walk to the pit with his friend Billy who lived almost opposite him. He'd pick up his lamp from the lamp cabin and take his place in the queue for the cage. The first day that he went into the cage he thought he was going to mess his pants. So many bodies kept climbing into the small space that he felt he couldn't breathe, he was so squashed. Sixteen or not, he wanted to yell for his Mam as the cage began to drop. It got blacker and blacker as the pale morning light vanished from his view. The cage swung from side to side and lowered in jerky movements and the air grew cooler and cooler until he shivered. It landed with a jolt and delivered him into the bowels of the earth.

He soon developed strong muscles in his new role of putter. He had to keep the hewers he worked with supplied with empty tubs and load their cut coal into them. Once they were filled to the brim he had to haul them along the long stretch of the seam back to the bottom of the shaft. Each tub weighed about ten hundred weight and each putter was expected to 'put' about fifty in a seven and a half hour shift. He had the help of his pit pony, with its trimmed mane and tail, to haul the stream of tubs along the seam. He loved his pony and built up a great rapport with it, much to the amusement of his mates.

Jimmy was never destined to be a tall man but at times being small was an advantage in the pit, as some of the seams - and they could stretch for a few miles - were only the width and height of a tub. But before he'd built up his muscular strength the huge and heavy fire doors proved to be a problem. A big fan at the top of the south shaft blew air down into the pit while the fan at the north shaft sucked it out to keep a constant flow of ventilation. A series of fire doors kept down the risk of spreading fire in the case of an explosion. Watching Jimmy hang from the big metal handles, as he tried to prise the doors open by pushing his feet against the wall and pulling to release the suction, became a great source of amusement for his marras.

The sense of comradeship down the pit was very strong. Jimmy soon learned the importance of trust in such a dangerous environment. It wasn't a case of every man for himself but more, 'I'll watch your back and you watch mine'. Friendships grew and developed underground over a period of time. A man's 'marra' was his workmate and the friend he'd do anything for.

Having missed out on a father-son relationship during his adolescent years Jimmy learned the facts of life working among the rare and honest breed of men. He found himself in the midst of a motley crew; some pious and highly religious, some crude and vulgar, but all looking out for one another. He lost all sense of modesty as he watched men strip naked as they worked in hot, stifling areas, or shit on the ground in a vacant spot. He'd heard some of the bluest jokes and some of the best singing as one man began to sing a hymn or song and the rest of them joined in. He learnt some swear words that his mother would have knocked his block off for repeating if he'd ever dared, but he never did. He learnt about real life in the great training world underground.

He had continued to go to Sunday school in Blackhall, just as he had at the Waterworks. He went with Edwin Bradley and Billy from his council estate and by the time they reached sixteen the Primitive Methodist Chapel was the centre of their social lives. There was something on almost every night of the week such as choir practices, concert rehearsals, Christian instruction sessions and the Christian endeavour where all the youths got together.

Jimmy was no saint however and if mischief was being done he was usually at the heart of it. He and Billy were chased for miles one night after they'd crumpled some newspapers and put them up the bottom of a metal drainpipe and set fire to it. It set off a noise that grew to a tremendous crescendo as the paper rose to the top of the pipe and blew it out letting off a siren. Other times they'd been known to take the hinges off gates and remove the bricks supporting a water butt so that the poor, unsuspecting person who came to fill their bucket with water got drenched as the butt lost its balance. It was harmless fun and they made sure nobody ever got hurt, but when Lizzie found out about such pranks Jimmy felt her wrath.

Lizzie was strict. As a single mother with adolescent youngsters she had to be. She was an upright, moral, God-fearing woman with strong principles, a private nature, terrific sense of humour and a heart full of love for her children. She adored young Jimmy and the thought of any harm coming to him was abhorrent to her. No matter that he was in his late teens, when it came to nine o'clock at night she'd open her front door to call him. She could see him, gathered with his friends under the street lamp in the cul-de-sac on Tweddle Crescent. 'Time to come in now Jimmy', she'd call, and he always obeyed her.

She hadn't wanted him to work in the pit; coming herself from a mining family she knew how it was for the men. But there was no alternative, and the free coal allowance would be a great help. She consoled herself, as she entered his name on the list at the colliery offices on East Street, that Blackhall was a modern pit. Mining had moved on here from the days when her Dad had worked every hour under the sun and come home black from head to foot. In the year before Jim died life was made far easier for the miners and their wives.

The Miners' Welfare Scheme, a fund for the improvement of social conditions for colliery workers, required a payment of one penny a ton from the coal mined during the previous year as part of the colliery's working expenses. Money from the fund at Blackhall paid for the building of the baths. When the buzzer sounded throughout the village, signifying the end of a shift, many mothers sent their little boys to the pithead to meet their Dads and nip into the shower with them. Much hearty singing could be heard from the showers as men revelled in the feel of hot water running down their backs. The air filled with bubbles from the zealous rubbing of soap against skin as coal-coloured water ran in rivulets into the drains. An area was provided for the men to grease their boots with fat as well as lockers to store their working clothes. No more need a pitman's wife or mother stand in the backyard and give her man's work clothes a good 'daddin' by beating them hard against the brick wall. Men could walk home through the cobbled streets sparkly clean, and embrace their loved ones before dinner.

Jimmy made deep and lasting friendships at the chapel with the group that had grown up through Sunday school. They became known as the 'gang'. The gang did everything together in their spare time. On Saturdays they'd go for bike rides and picnics. They'd swim in the sea at Blackhall Rocks, but there was a risk of whirlpools there and as Jimmy had almost lost his life as he began to get sucked into one they decided that Seaton Carew was the safer place. They would often walk along the Coast Road to Crimdon Dene and while away sun-filled days on the golden sands. They had fun and enjoyed one another's company. Edwin and Jimmy were inseparable at times and became as close as brothers. Jimmy was always welcomed into the Bradley home where he was treated in the same way as Bob and Freda's own three children.

Jimmy and Edwin were fun loving and great instigators of monkey business. But between them sitting on the front row of the chapel's balcony, reading the *Beano* and tearing off corners of its paper to screw up into little balls and drop onto the hats below them, the messages being preached seeped through. In the darkness of the pit Jimmy found the God that was to shape his life. In the Christian endeavour group, he found the love of his life. One of his friends appealed to his better nature and asked him to fix him up with a date with the sweet and painfully shy Irene. Jimmy approached the quiet girl with the skinny legs, but as they got talking, for the first time on a real one to one basis, he became captivated. He noticed her pretty, silvery, grey-green eyes and bewitchingly cute smile. He forgot all about his friend and asked her to go to the pictures with him on Friday night.

They began to spend a lot of time together, walking along the beach and sheltering from the fierce winds on the cliff tops. Irene was an assiduous young lady who loved Jimmy's spirit of fun while Jimmy loved Irene's serious nature and carefully tuned mind. Instead of leaving school at fourteen Irene had won a scholarship to go to Henry Smith's grammar school along with Jimmy's sister Betty and Gwennie before her.

Jimmy grew very intense about God. With his sense of humour still intact he began to grow and mature in a new direction. He heard no mighty voice calling from the heavens and no angelic music raining down from the sky. Neither did any vision of God or Jesus appear before his eyes. But he did feel a sense of being 'pulled' into the direction of the ministry. The thought kept turning up in his head and wouldn't leave him alone. His jaw ached with a constant grinding of his teeth as he played with the idea. 'Me, in a dog collar? It's a ridiculous picture, why am I even thinking about it?' He rebuked himself crossly as he manoeuvred a heavy tub onto the rail. 'I was useless at school, how can I stand up amongst clever men in college? Who'll take me, a daft pit lad, seriously?' But still the idea plagued his dreams and doubts confused his wakefulness.

Slowly, like tomatoes growing on a vine and ripening red in the sun, Jimmy's heart began to flutter and stir with hope. Feelings of love filled his days. 'I can preach love', he mused. 'I don't want to stand in a pulpit and breathe hellfire and brimstone, scaring folk to death, I want to preach love'. With his lips pursed, eyes screwed and chin tilted, he pondered the possibilities. 'Maybe I can help people', he nodded in response to his own notions.

When he voiced his thoughts to Irene he found she was receptive to them. However, when he mentioned his intentions to a wider circle of people, beyond the gang, he was almost laughed out of town. Lizzie questioned his academic ability, but not his heart. Some elder members of the chapel, and workmates at the pit couldn't get their heads around the daft nineteen-year-old who thought he had the intelligence to be able to study at the degree necessary to qualify as a Methodist minister. Those who had witnessed his pranks and clipped his ears in punishment sniggered as they shook their heads. But none of them were prepared for little Jimmy's depth of sheer grit and determination.

One of the ministers in the local circuit did take him seriously and offered his full support. The kindly Reverend saw a spark in Jimmy and counselled him in the way to go forward. The first thing to do was to get some general education and 'O' levels under his belt. Then to go on 'note' as a local preacher which meant further studies in the Old and New Testaments of the Bible as well as Christian doctrines. Then he could start to have a go at writing sermons. Jimmy quelled the sickening fear rising in his stomach and the panic, hammering in his chest, caused by the daunting project ahead. He arranged a regular payment, to be deducted from his wage packets, to grant him the use of the colliery's reading room.

On the first Sunday morning that he was booked down to preach he got out of bed very early. He carefully tamed his wavy, dark brown hair into its quiff before dressing in his only suit. With his notes in his hand he stood in front of the mirror and addressed his reflection. He spoke to himself clearly and in as posh an accent as he could muster. Once at the chapel, after praying in the vestry with the steward on duty, he walked to the pulpit on legs like jelly. He made it up the steps and gave a great big smile to the whole congregation that lit up his lean, handsome face. 'Good morning everybody', he boomed in a voice that seemed to be coming from somewhere else. After an opening hymn he delivered his three point sermon with all thoughts of a posh accent forgotten. A familiar face, sitting directly in his line of vision, raised his hand to his breast pocket and took out a shiny gold pocket-watch from his waistcoat. He looked at it pointedly and gave a little cough.

But Jimmy could not be deterred. Eventually people came to realise that the conscientious approach he applied to his studies was going to carry him through. He gained strength from their support and the depth of his sermons eventually won their respect. The Bradley family did whatever they could to help him and paid for some books. Irene diligently coached him in his mathematics. Lizzie and his sisters positively shone with pride and whispered around the house so that he could have some peace and quiet while studying.

From the first day that Jimmy had begun work at the pit Lizzie had reserved the best food for him. He'd always been a fast eater, having learned from an early age that to dawdle over food meant that it got picked off his plate by one of his sisters. Imagine his glee when he got home from work, bone tired and aching from head to foot, to find a whole meat and potato pie being put in front of him fresh from the oven. As soon as he cleared a space on the plate his Mam filled it with fresh garden peas. Margaret and Betty watched him eat every mouthful and pleaded for a taste. Jimmy grinned as he taunted them.

On the Monday night following his previous day's first preached sermon, the smile was wiped from his face. 'Now Jimmy', said Lizzie, 'once you're a minister you can't scoop your peas up onto your fork'.

'Well how else can I get them to my mouth?' he queried as he began to stab them with the prongs.

'No you can't do that either, you have to use your knife

to push them onto the top of the fork and balance them'.

'But they just roll off', he protested.

'Well you'll just have to keep practising', she insisted. Jimmy vowed, in his holiness, to abstain from peas.

PIT TO PULPIT

The village of Blackhall lies in two parts, the Colliery at the top northern end, with Middle Street as its main thoroughfare leading in a straight line onto Coast Road and the dormitory village of Blackhall Rocks with its wild beach banks. Whoops of joy echoed from the Colliery to the Rocks and even the local newspapers declared the good news. Jimmy had been accepted as a candidate for the Ministry. His intense studies had paid off. After almost eight years of working as a miner in the pit he was about to turn the tide of his future. During the Second World War he'd raced to the war office to sign up for the Royal Navy, but had been refused. Under Ernest Bevin's scheme (the then Minister of Labour) to produce more coal for the war effort, he'd been ordered to continue hauling tubs as a 'Bevin boy'. Now, he was about to leave the darkness of the underground and see the light.

He asked Irene to marry him. He'd rehearsed his speech a thousand times but on the night he'd planned to propose the words just wouldn't come out. They stood outside her front door to say goodnight as usual and every time Irene turned to go in Jimmy asked her to stay another minute. For an hour and a half he shifted from foot to foot, rattled the coins in his jacket pocket and concentrated his vision on an invisible spot on the ground. Eventually, instead of dropping to one knee as he'd practised he blurted out, 'So, how about it then?' 'How about what?' she giggled. 'How about us...you know...getting married?' Phew, he'd done it and of course she said yes.

After a series of medical examinations, one of which he scraped through, Jimmy received the letter informing him of his place in theological college. At the time of the tests he'd fallen victim to the miner's disease known as Nystagmus, the symptoms of which are headaches, dizziness and oscillation of the eyeballs. Fortunately the doctor performing the examination was familiar with the problem and so not deterred by the young man whose eyeballs rolled around in their sockets as he dropped his trousers to cough.

At the age of twenty-one Jimmy left his beloved Mam and sisters to board the train from Hartlepool to Manchester. He was a humble star in the village and the first member of his chapel to enter the ministry. Proud friends and neighbours waved him off to begin a new and unfamiliar life of academia.

Irene also was embarking on a new life. Since leaving school, with a thick wad of ordinary and advanced certificates, she had worked for the highly respected Dr. Russell. He'd painstakingly trained her in the art of dispensing his prescribed pills and tonics with the notion that she'd serve him well into the future. When she informed the doctor of her decision to join her elder sister Doris and train as a nurse he looked at his full shelves of medicines and groaned at the prospect of training a new recruit.

Irene was naive and easily shocked. Astonishment filled her being as she came into contact with girls her own age who were neither married nor betrothed and yet were having sex with men. 'But it's wrong', she'd protest to Doris who, having already completed her first year of training, had adjusted to the goings on in certain quarters of the nurses' block. Doris had the task of calming her delicate little sister down. Calm and adjust she did and got stuck into a life of nursing that she soon came to love. She even made friends with some of the more 'forward' girls who looked at her askance when she vowed that she and Jimmy would 'wait' until they were married. 'But it's going to be six years until you're allowed to get married', they protested. (Ministers were not allowed to marry until they were fully ordained following two years of college and three years' probation). 'We'll still wait', she affirmed.

Separated by many miles, with Jimmy in Manchester and Irene at Newcastle General Hospital, their courtship depended on letters. They wrote reams to each other daily. Jimmy found a new interest in poetry and often recited love poems by Shakespeare and Spenser, adding many written through his own inspiration. He loved his life at Hartley Victoria College and engaged in much fun and hilarity with a new circle of clerical friends. But his devotion to his 'calling' never diminished. In one letter he asked Irene to pray for him regarding approaching exams. He wrote, 'I have no further interest in life if I cannot preach the gospel of Christ Jesus my Lord. Few people seem to understand me, but I trust that you do my love?'

He did pass all his exams, although the elocution lessons had seriously challenged him. He was fiercely protective of his Durham accent and proud of it too. But he had had to admit that occasionally he faced a congregation who sat with bewildered expressions on their faces as he preached. His first placement as a probationary minister was near Barnsley. As he was introduced, wearing his very first dog collar, he thought he would burst with pride. The only down side to his time there was his lodgings.

While Irene shared a nice comfortable room with Doris, he rented a drab and miserable room with Miss Higginsbottom. She was an old spinster of indefinable age. She wore her long grey hair scraped severely back into a bun and an apron over her drab woollen skirts and two-pieces. Penny pinching was an art she excelled in and her sharp eyes never missed a trick. She switched the electricity off at eight o'clock in the evenings, leaving Jimmy to write his sermons and preparations by the light of his torch. She counted each piece of loo roll between the perforated lines and charged for each piece used. But the real cracker was when Jimmy came 'home' with a portion of fresh tripe, a treat for his supper. 'I've already prepared your supper so you'll have to leave that for tomorrow', she insisted. Jimmy had wanted to eat it while it was still fresh but he knew there was no use in protesting. He sat at the table and looked in dismay at the cold, dried up kipper full of bones she put in front of him with a couple of slices of bread and butter. He chewed on the tasteless morsel with regret and after washing up his plate and cutlery went to his room to work. He'd forgotten his notebook and went back to the table to retrieve it. His face was a picture as he walked into the kitchen to see old Higginsbottom eating his tripe.

He needed some light relief every now and again from the demands of his new role and that came in the form of Edwin Bradley. He fell back into his old accent and became Jimmy from the colliery with ease whenever he was visited by him. They both had a passion for motorcycles. Jimmy had bought an old Norton bike with a side-car attached, given to him at an exceptionally low price by Bob Bradley. As well as being the check-weighman at the colliery Bob was a bit of an entrepreneur. He earned a good wage at his job and saved enough money to buy two black limousines to create the only taxi service in and around Blackhall. They were just the beginning of the garage and motor sales empire he later built up with his sons Edwin and Ernest. Edwin arranged to take Jimmy to a motorcycle convention in London. He would get on the train at Darlington and Jimmy had to make sure he got on the same one at Barnsley. As he stood on the platform he saw Edwin's round, smiling face and neatly cut, golden hair as he leaned out, waving, from the carriage window. Jimmy climbed aboard and was greeted by a rowdy group of motorcycle enthusiasts who were also heading for the convention. 'This is the Rev. Jimmy Parkinson', Edwin proudly introduced his friend to the group he'd been chatting with on the journey. 'Ay and I'm the bloody Bishop of Leeds', one of the men threw back towards the unlikely looking clergyman in his flat cap.

Jimmy loved his motorbike with a passion because it gave him a sense of freedom, and taking it for a ride helped to clear his mind. But he couldn't always afford to buy the petrol to run it so he had an old second-hand bicycle as well, a sit-up-and-beg Lucas. When his two years at Barnsley came to an end he said his 'fond' farewell to Miss Higginsbottom and moved on to his next appointment in Rotherham. He was more fortunate with his lodgings this time and parked his bike and cycle outside the home where he was treated as one of the family.

He put his cycle to good use to boost his meagre income by delivering meat for the local butcher on Saturday mornings. Filling the front basket he knocked on doors and handed over the Sunday roasting joints with a beaming smile, cheering housewives immensely and ensuring their seat on a pew the following morning. Then with enough money to buy petrol he'd jump onto his motorbike and whizz to Rotherham's hospital where Irene, now a fully qualified State Registered Nurse, had got a job to be near him. Sister Irene Robinson and Reverend Jimmy Parkinson had eyes for no one but each other, despite the attentions they received from starry-eyed young ladies and dashing young doctors.

Back at home the Blackhall gang were pairing up and walking down the aisle in holy matrimony. Poor Irene was always the bridesmaid but never the bride. It was hard for them, watching their friends arrange weddings and begin family life. But there was nothing they could do until Jimmy's probationary period was complete, and at least they had other plans to occupy their minds. Irene's decision to train as a nurse was for reasons beyond following in her sister's trail.

When Jimmy and Irene returned to Blackhall for a holiday they announced their intention to offer themselves for the mission fields of India. Gasps resounded and arms clasped tightly around chests. It shouldn't have come as such a huge surprise, as Jimmy had always talked of his desire to be a missionary. But to hear that they had already begun to set the ball rolling, on condition of Jimmy's successful ordination, was a harsh reality their families didn't want to face. 'But how will they have babies in India?' queried the gang.

The day of ordination loomed. It was to be held in Birmingham's Central Hall during the summer month of July. Jimmy was a happy chappie indeed as he signed the papers for the hired car he'd booked and set off back to Blackhall from Rotherham to collect his Mam and sisters. His sisters, all married by now, were highly excitable girls. Gwennie was perhaps the most serious of the four. Ella, with her dark exotic features and shiny black hair, never stopped talking. Margaret, who had a round, pretty face and red hair was a bundle of joy and loved by everyone. Betty was shamefully beautiful and turned every head that she passed.

The two middle girls were accompanying Jimmy to Birmingham. Jimmy opened the door of the old Ford model T and the sisters squeezed into the back seat and made themselves comfortable. Lizzie, dressed in the new pale blue suit she'd made especially for the occasion, secured the long pin into her hat and stepped gracefully into the front passenger seat. The long journey passed, accompanied by Ella's dulcet tones. Margaret occasionally responded to her with an 'Eee, well I never', or 'Uh huh, um, yes', as she passed round a bag of sweets. Lizzie looked out of the window and raised her hand to wave, as would the Queen, to all passersby.

In Birmingham they met Irene off her train from Rotherham, and together they made their way to the vast Central Hall. Margaret, whose geography was not the best, wondered if she'd get a glimpse of Big Ben. They each hugged and kissed Jimmy as they separated and the four women found their allotted seats. They each held their breath as they caught sight of him making his way along the procession with his fellow ordinands. Tears rolled down Lizzie's cheeks when she heard her son's name being read out and watched him shake hands and take the Bible from the president of the conference, the Reverend Donald Oliver Soper. Little Jimmy's eyes sought out those of his dearest Mam, lovely sisters and very soon to be wife up in the balcony, and he winked with a huge smile on his face. 'If only my Dad could see me now', he thought as he clutched his newly presented Bible and rubbed his arms to make sure his shirt sleeves were still rolled up beneath his jacket. It was the only way he knew to keep the memory of his Dad alive.

COLD TEA AND A RAILWAY BENCH

Lizzie Parkinson and May Robinson had never really seen eye to eye, but when their children got together, forming a link between them, they both did their best to accommodate one another. Lizzie was a very private woman who kept her own counsel and had no time for busy-bodies. She would stand in the longest queue at the bank or shop if she thought the assistant at the end of the shortest queue might be interested in her business. She'd known a hard life since the death of her husband and had become adept at managing her meagre finances. She put money aside in little boxes and tins, and notes were hidden under her mattresses and between the pages of carefully folded newspapers. She had an alert mind and a sharp memory and never forgot where that ten bob note, reserved for emergencies was.

May was born in a house overlooking Haworth Moor. Her Yorkshire up-bringing, amidst the spinners and weavers of worsted in the mills of Keighley, remained a dominant element of her character. She was a staunch chapelite and a leader, taking an active role in the organisation of events and activities. Many of the cups, saucers, cake tins and cutlery in her house sported a little sticker on the bottom with the initials, M.J.R., Mary Jane Robinson, so that the women in the chapel's kitchen knew which pile to stack them in. She was a good actress and quite the comedian in pantomimes, and she had many friends. She was also, at times, a rather formidable lady. Woe betide anybody who bought an ice cream on a Sunday and got spotted by May.

Both May and Lizzie were women of loyalty when it came to giving their undivided custom to the fair trading co-operative store in grateful thanks for the downfall of the colliery controlled Tommy shops. In the earlier days of pit life the colliery ruled the roost of the entire village built up around it. Communities developed around the mines that were often sunk in remote areas. Houses were hastily put up, with little consideration paid to style and practicality and lacking in any degree of panache. The only shop available to the miners and their families was either run by the mine or a close relative of the colliery owner. Miners received their wages, their wives spent them in the shop and the profits came back into the mine in a convenient little circle. In many cases deductions were even made in the wages prior to (under-weighed) purchases, giving the colliery complete control over its people.

May's husband, Ernie, had a heart warming smile and a gentleness that belied his physical strength. He worked quietly and solidly at his hewing and was never known to grumble, in or out of the pit. On a day when a full tub of coal de-railed, leaving his young putter in a flap and a quandary, Ernie went to his rescue. As he bent down to man-handle the heavy tub back onto its rail he caught three of his fingers between the wheel and the rail. Blood gushed from his fingers and the young lad's face turned green as he vomited the bait he'd just eaten. Ernie saw to the boy and made him drink a swill of water before wrapping his own butchered fingers in his sooty handkerchief and returning to work with his pick. It was the way he was.

May had not really approved of the young Jimmy and his ever performing pranks. But as his intentions of becoming a minister began to take fruition, and she saw her daughter's future as a parson's wife, she decided that she could put up with him even if he was Lizzie Parkinson's son. She'd barely had time to take a breath and turn herself around after her eldest daughter, Doris's, wedding before she began running up and down Middle Street ordering flowers and invitations for Irene's.

It had been a summer worthy of May's fastidious organisational skills. Amidst the hubbub of merry street parties in honour of Queen Elizabeth the second's coronation she had flourished. Her flowery cotton aprons held a tight rein on her ample bosoms as she flitted between a hot oven, where her fairy cakes rose resplendent, and her notebook laden with lists of things to do.

Lizzie's house was no more relaxed in atmosphere as she sat bent over her Singer sewing machine. Pressing the exhausted foot pedal for all its worth she fed length upon length of material along the machine's shiny black surface as the needle hopped its way through frothy white organdie and net. Ella, Margaret and Betty buzzed in and out of the house, standing each of their sons on the kitchen table to be measured for pageboy outfits.

Ernie Robinson sat in his rocking-chair with a cup of tea and wondered how Irene, with her sweet elfin face, was going to get on living in India. He'd never even seen a man, woman or child with brown skin and he'd never heard of curry. He was a man who thrived on routine and liked to eat meat with two veg. He was worried about his little girl and what would become of her. He loved Jimmy though, and knew that he would cherish her. 'I'll just have to hope and pray that they'll be alright', he thought, as May blustered past him with yet another tray full of cups and saucers he was ordered to take up to the chapel.

Jimmy's probation in Rotherham had come to an end and he bade an emotional farewell to the members of his congregation and the energetic youth group in the newly built Chapel at Broom. He sent his old Lucas and a parcel of books home by rail and picked Irene up on his motorbike. She too had worked out her notice at the hospital where she'd made many friends with colleagues and patients alike. She was a deeply caring nurse and often went above and beyond the call of duty to ensure her patients' welfare. During the last week of her employment a group of them had arranged a song to be played for her over the radio. With glistening eyes she stopped short in her bed making as she heard her name read out and the song, '*Stay as sweet as you are*', sung especially for her, by Nat 'King' Cole.

Jimmy collected Irene on his motorbike and the lovebirds set off on their return to Blackhall, and their long awaited wedding day. Settled snugly into the side-car she smiled up at him with his round goggles covering his eyes and a helmet strapped under his chin. It was a long journey, before the days of motorways, and Irene needed to spend a penny. She waved her arms and tapped on the window trying to attract his attention but Jimmy, intent on his driving, remained oblivious. When he finally stopped to put some petrol in the tank he found, to his dismay, a sobbing Irene in dire straits and urgent need of a ladies' convenience. He learnt his first lesson in tuning in to the needs of a wife there and then.

Children gathered in clusters outside number thirty-seven Tenth Street. They whooped and clapped as Irene came out of her front door, a dazzling display in white. As she got into the back seat of one of the Bradleys' shiny black cars with her father, the children raced along beside it to the chapel. The distance between the house and the chapel was only a stone's throw, but the driver wove through the back streets of terraced houses to add drama to the occasion. Ernie counted the blocks of houses from one to ten. Each row of terraces was named, literally in the order in which it had been built, First Street, Second Street, Third Street and so on. Most of the houses faced south towards the Rocks and the street behind faced the back door of the one in front. They didn't reach Eleventh Street as the chapel was in the middle of Tenth Street where it was intersected by Middle Street.

The children got to the chapel before the car and shouted its imminent arrival. Ernie held tightly to Irene's hand and wiped his eyes with the clean handkerchief that May had insisted upon. 'You look a picture hinny', he whispered to her in a choked voiced. 'Thank you Daddy', she beamed, 'I love you'.

May was all smiles as she watched her second daughter walk down the aisle in her long, flowing organdie dress and veil. She saw her hands shake as they clutched the bouquet of pink roses and sweetly fragranced lily of the valley. Doris too looked beautiful, carrying the bouquet of white dahlias and gladioli, to set off the pale green of her dress. 'If only Ronnie could be here to see her', May thought, as she pictured her youngest child, Irene and Doris's adored little brother, looking smart and dashing in his uniform of the Royal Navy.

The two pageboys looked endearing dressed in white satin flouncy shirts and dark green satin trousers. But one boy was missing, there should have been three. Ella tutted as she held onto her son Ian's hand. Little Ian hadn't fancied the idea at all, of being all done up in satin like a doll at Christmas, so he'd cut a big chunk of hair out of his fringe to escape the humiliation. Poor Ella looked crestfallen when Betty's son Glyn, and Margaret's son Keith, stole the show.

Jimmy, standing at the front of the chapel next to Edwin, his best man, gaped in awe at his lovely Irene as she floated down the aisle. Lizzie, standing quietly with her excited daughters and their husbands, smiled a gentle smile at the happiness on her son's face. It was the son that she idolized and thanked the good Lord for. 'But why do you have to send him to the other side of the world to do your work?' she questioned God with admonishment.

Long trestle tables were laid in the Sunday school room at the back of the Chapel. Small vases of lily of the valley adorned the starched white tablecloths and kettles whistled their tunes at boiling point. Plates stacked high with ham sandwiches sat next to big dishes of cold pease pudding. The Methodist bun fight was a jolly affair, and as Edwin rapped his spoon on the table to quieten the rabble, ladies rushed around filling glasses with cold tea for the toasts. In true Methodist fashion alcohol was strictly abstained from and not a drop came past the threshold.

The shiny black car was again on hand to transport the newly-weds to the station to hop on board the train to Bristol. Dressed in a new cream suit, Irene smiled coyly at her husband and the couple shared their eagerness for the moment when they arrived at the caravan in Devon and they could, at last, consummate their love. Alas, the train pulled onto Bristol station at twenty minutes passed midnight, just as their connecting train to Devon pulled away. Aghast, they went in search of a hotel to spend a few hours until early morning when they were due to catch the next train to Exeter at six forty-five. There was no room available at any Inn so they had no choice but to snuggle up on a bench in the station's waiting room. For nine years, in total, they had been courting their love and stemming their desire for one another. For one more night they were just going to have to continue to wait.

They spent a glorious honeymoon in the cosy caravan, where the two became one at last. Irene also discovered, with alarm, a few of Jimmy's less appealing habits of untidiness in the confines of such a small space. The act of real sharing began. But as soon as the holiday ended they again packed their suitcases and moved into the married quarters of the missionary training and language school in Selly Oak, Birmingham. They spent a year there, learning about the different cultures and religions of India as well as the all-important language of Hindi, their tool of communication. Alongside cultural studies the trainee missionaries travelled around the Birmingham district taking services to fulfil their ministerial obligations. So they were left with very little spare time in which to reflect upon the enormity of what lay ahead.

Equipped with their new knowledge and perceptions of India, Jimmy and Irene held a captive audience back home amongst their friends and families. Lizzie looked, open-mouthed, at Jimmy as he baffled her with his grasp of Hindi. The sisters giggled uncontrollably as they listened to incomprehensible words coming from their brother's mouth. A similar scene took place in Tenth Street as the Robinsons gathered around the tea table to listen to Irene's equally mystifying tales.

The month of August celebrated Jimmy and Irene's first wedding anniversary, but otherwise it passed in a flurry of preparation. People all over the country longed to feel warm sunshine on their skin and turn their eyes to clear blue skies. Rain had prevailed throughout the year and thunderstorms rumbled in from the sea as May and Lizzie's orderly houses turned into scenes reminiscent of a chapel jumble sale. Irene stacked piles of clothes, bed linen, towels and toiletries across tables and chairs and Jimmy sorted books and papers. Trunks stood open in bedrooms and were packed and unpacked in indecision of what would and would not be needed. Lizzie shook her head in wonder as she watched Jimmy hammer hundreds of nails into a wooden crate of books. Just to make sure his precious collection was secure he finished off with a few dozen screws.

As the day of departure approached Lizzie grew more anxious. She'd already said goodbye to her eldest daughter, Gwennie, who had married a white South African man during the war. But at least she had gone to a lush land and a beautiful house in Johannesburg with fruit trees in the garden (Lizzie wasn't too clued up on the massive problems of apartheid that affected the country). That didn't make up for how much she missed her, but at least she felt she was safe and happy and could speak in her own tongue. 'Eee Jimmy', she thought, 'will you have a fruit tree in your garden pet?'

Newspapers around the county of Durham again declared their news as headlines announced, *'Leaving for the Mission Field'*, *'Blackhall Couple's Venture'* and simply *'Farewell'*. An article following the valedictory service held in their honour recorded the farewell dedication speech made by their minister in which he wished them well and prayed for their safety and work. *'A Parting Gift'*, described the gleaming canteen of cutlery in a polished wooden box presented to them, as a token of affection and goodwill, by the members of their chapel.

Edwin drove Jimmy and Irene with Lizzie, May and Ernie to London to catch the Waterloo boat train to Southampton. Everybody came out onto the street in Blackhall to wave them off. Emotions were running high, and it wasn't just the women who sniffed into their hankies. The brothers-in-law all felt the weight of loss; they and Jimmy had been very close friends and members of the chapel 'gang'. It was the same with Irene and the sisters. Betty's husband, George, Margaret's husband Joe and Ella's husband Charlie, they'd all grown up together in the small community. Doris stood with her husband, another Jimmy, the handsome pathologist she'd met while nursing. Hugs and kisses passed freely around the group gathered on Tenth Street. Men slapped each other on the back affectionately. Ernie, being the strong, silent type, kept his heartache in check and lent his support to May and Lizzie as the car drove smoothly along Coast Road and away from Blackhall.

Jimmy and Irene pushed down the window in the door of the train and leaned out to wave. Their faces were alight with smiles and wet with tears as they began to move slowly away from the station platform in a cloud of hissing steam. Edwin squared his shoulders, but his face turned red as the friend he'd shared tears and laughter with over the years disappeared from his sight. The bereft parents stared into the distance following the line of the empty track. A gripping pain of loss clutched their hearts. The young couple on the train held each other tightly and wept.

At Southampton they were relieved to find that their trunks and crates, sent on ahead of them, had been stored as cargo on board the ship. They passed through customs without a problem before walking up the gang plank onto the SS Canton, of the Peninsular and Oriental Steam Navigation Company. A steward led them to cabin number

336/7 which, from the eighteenth day of September 1954, was to be their home for the next two weeks. They put down their luggage and went up on deck. The wind blew through their hair as they viewed the huge stretch of sea that lay ahead of them, and England's comforting shore as it gently dwindled on the horizon.

JUST A LITTLE SIGN

I spent a few hours familiarising myself with the county of Durham and as I drove and walked I found it hard to imagine a landscape once blotted with pitheads and driving wheels. Acres of fields, in many shades of green, stretched far and wide displaying fresh and open views. Where at one time, in the throngs of the coal mining industry the land was powdered in black soot, it now glows with nature's soft, gentle hues. The air these days is calm and clear, filled with a natural scent, devoid now of the ever-present smoke that churned from tall chimneys, catching the back of people's throats and stinging their eyes. The deafening drone of engine houses, working all day and throughout the night, creating a stressful barrage of noise, can no longer be heard. All was peaceful and beautiful in my sight that morning. I was cold and hungry when I arrived in Blackhall but my intention of finding somewhere to enjoy a healthy lunch evaporated the moment I breathed the seductive aroma of fish and chips. At the top of the road leading down to the beach banks at Blackhall Rocks stood three shops. I was drawn to the one 'now frying' as if in a trance.

    I took my piping hot parcel onto the cliff tops and savoured each mouthful of fresh fish in its light crispy batter.

The chunky chips, crispy on the outside and soft and fluffy within, lifted me onto a whole new realm of ecstasy. The flavours were further enhanced as they mingled with the smell of fresh, salty sea air. So very strange, I thought, as I scooped a small wooden fork full of mushy peas into my mouth, to imagine that beneath these rocks lay long tunnels along which men had laboured to collect coal. I find it odd to imagine a young Jimmy pulling and pushing heavy tubs in the dark, lighting his way with his Davy lamp, so deep underground and perhaps a mile or so out below the sea. Was he praying and planning, whistling as he led his pony along a narrow seam? Many of his workmates swore at their ponies to get them to oblige but he never could, he preferred to cajole and encourage the sensitive animal that never saw the light of day. For the briefest moment I felt myself down there with him, freezing cold and claustrophobic; the thought made me shiver as I dropped my paper wrapping into a litter bin.

The plight of the hard-grafting, brave men who mined coal to keep the country ticking along, but who were never properly credited for the risks they took on a daily basis, hit me hard as I looked out to sea. It's one thing to look at a black and white photograph of men, smiling in the dark, their eyes and teeth gleaming against the blackness of the coal. But to look from this standpoint and think of them descending into the bowels of the earth, beneath incalculable weights of water and rock, is quite another.

It was on these rugged, limestone cliff banks, amidst thick bracken and wild rough grass that Jimmy and Irene had sat in their youth. Wrapped in each other's arms they'd gazed out across the North Sea, watching the aerial ropeway dump its twenty-eight half ton buckets of colliery waste out to sea, and shared their dreams and visions of a joint future.

The ropeway, that saved Blackhall from having a sooty and unsightly spoil heap at its heart but made a mess of the sea, is gone now, dismantled with the closure of the pit. Regeneration programmes have taken place across the county and the beaches and sea have been cleaned up. Here the cliff tops have been transformed into a nature reserve, along with many of the other colliery sites. It's a beautiful area, a wild and rugged natural sanctuary for birds, butterflies and flowers. I can imagine that many young lovers still enjoy the peaceful surroundings. Indeed, I see a red hatchback parked at the far corner of the car park with misty windows.

I know where the mine used to stand here, having spent many a summer holiday with my beloved Auntie Margaret, Uncle Joe and my grandmothers. But for new visitors, and myself in other villages, I can't help wishing that something, just a little sign perhaps, had been put in place to signify the spot on which it stood. A worthy mark of pride to show respect to the many thousands of men (and women in the early days) who worked in hazardous and ghastly conditions stands in the main street: the pit's driving wheel is mounted, as witness to the history of the village. I like that.

After a brisk walk along the beach, to burn off a few fish and chip calories, I walked up the hill, along Ocean View and round the corner to Tweddle Crescent and the house on the corner plot. The house from where Jimmy left home to go to college and to where I was brought to live for a while after my birth in the hospital at what was then called West Hartlepool. I passed the cemetery, in the dead centre of Blackhall on my way to the colliery and went in to see if I could find the grave of Jimmy's father, the grandfather I never knew. Knowing it was originally unmarked, I searched for an indication of his burial plot that may have been added at a later date. I found none but noted the address of a man who may be able to help me.

I stood outside a shop on Middle Street and looked up at the windows of the flat where little Jimmy first heard about the death of his Dad and passed the Co-operative store before crossing the road to the colliery houses, now privately owned. Such a practical, yet unimaginative way to name streets, in simple numerical order, but it does lend a certain appeal. The pit used to stand at the bottom end of these streets so most of the men didn't have very far to walk to work. Many a chorus of clopping boots will have echoed from these roads in the early hours of the mornings and again at the end of each shift. I walked along West Street, where Irene was born, and the length of Tenth Street where she later lived, and allowed my gaze to linger on the spot where Jimmy, awkwardly, proposed marriage. These houses didn't have bathrooms or even running water in her day, just a cold tap in the small scullery and a privy in the back yard.

I visited some friends of the young Jimmy and Irene, former members of the chapel gang, who regaled me with stories of their youth. They told me that Jimmy was an intense young lad but that he always had a big grin on his face. 'If Jimmy Parkinson was around', they said, 'there was always fun to be had'. That was nice to hear. They took me into the chapel that was such an integral part of his life and encouraged me to walk up the stairs and stand in the pulpit where he delivered his very first sermon. I sat in the seat that Irene sat in, beaming with pride for her man. 'I don't think they could have survived their time in India', the friends asserted, 'and all the illness they endured, if they hadn't had such a sense of humour alongside their devotion'.

I had intended to walk the bank to Horden, but when I saw it I declined. It is a very steep bank so Jimmy's Dad must have been very fit, before being taken by tuberculosis, to have walked it so many times a day. I pictured the gang freewheeling down at high speed on their bicycles in the summer, then puffing hard as they pedalled up the steep incline. 'Irene', the friends told me, 'was a little dot of a thing with legs as skinny as a chicken's. But she cycled up that bank with ease'. They'd never understood how she did it. 'Jimmy', they said, used to ride back and forward to make sure that everyone struggling behind was alright'.

On my way back to the Rocks I passed Airlie House, first built by the doctor that Irene worked for in the days before the National Health Service. This is the building where she learnt to dispense prescriptions. I could almost hear Jimmy's yell still resounding from the surgery and out across the village. Just after he began work at the pit he broke his arm during a game of football. Doctor Russell told him a tale to distract him, laid the misshapen arm on his desk and with a sharp snap he reset the broken bone.

I checked the time and hurried back to the cemetery where I'd arranged to meet the man from the council. He took out his plan and led me to the plot where Jim Parkinson, Jimmy's father, was buried. He hammered a small stake of wood into the ground at the head of the grave to mark the spot, then discreetly walked away to leave me to my reflections. I can picture a little boy with dark brown hair, neatly combed across his head from a side parting. A little boy with big brown eyes like his mother's, standing wringing his fingers and looking, with a bewildered expression, from the coffin in the deep hole up to his mother's face for an explanation she cannot give. I feel my throat tightening as I think about him wondering what all the ceremony is about and what's going to happen next. I imagine him tugging the sleeve of his sister's coat and whispering, 'Is me Dad coming back?' then frowning as she shakes her head and whispers, 'No'.

I'd bought a bunch of daffodils, from a shop at the colliery, and took them back to the cliff tops. I made my way to the edge of the cliffs and found the spot where we'd gathered as a family, first with Mum and the second time without her, to scatter the ashes of my parents into the sea. I threw two stems off the cliff and lay the rest down by my feet in their memory. Who, or what, is this God that plucked a little putter from the pit and planted him in a pulpit, then sailed him way across the sea? Where are you now Mum and Dad? Are you living a new life after death or are you, simply, no more?

I remembered some of Dad's final words, he was in a particularly bad bout of pain when suddenly, he smiled, almost laughed and said, 'Eee, who'd imagine that God would want someone like me, little Jimmy Parkinson'. I know that morphine can have some strange effects on people, cause a state of euphoria, but there was something very moving about his words. God certainly allowed him to suffer. He didn't alleviate any pain or discomfort, and there were no visible benefits to the dying process after a lifetime's devotion that I could see. Jimmy's life was energized by a 'truth' that he felt was compelling and absolute. 'Who are you, what are you?' I whispered into the wind. 'Were Jimmy and Irene justified in following you throughout their days, or have they been had? After all they went through some pretty rough times'. 'Oh for a sign', I sighed as a seagull swooped low and let out a shrill squawk.

IN HUMBLE SERVICE

Jimmy hung his head over the rail on the top deck of the ship. Irene lay on the bed in the cabin clutching a metal bowl. Their complexions were a pale shade of green and their stomachs were empty and cramped. Nausea made their heads spin. The weather had been stormy and the sea choppy for three days since setting sail and the rocking motion on board was unrelenting.

Their glee at such a plentiful supply of food had got the better of them. At breakfast on the first morning afloat Jimmy had relished every course put in front of him. He'd begun with cereals, followed by an enormous plate full of bacon, eggs, sausages, beans, tomatoes, mushrooms and fried bread, finished off with toast and marmalade and a pot of tea. Morning coffee was provided only a short time later and served with cakes and biscuits. Halfway through the five course lunch, as the ship began to rise and fall, the soup and poached halibut had Jimmy running for the deck. After a few days, on a diet of dry toast and sips of water while sitting on deck-chairs in the fresh air, they both started to feel better.

They enjoyed excellent company with a group of fellow missionaries. Even though they travelled in tourist class,

Jimmy and Irene had never before experienced such levels of luxury. Glorious sunshine tanned their skin as they sailed over the beautiful blue waters of the Mediterranean. They spent blissful days swimming in the ship's pool and playing tennis on deck. Their appetites perked up after the spell of sea-sickness and their sunken cheeks plumped.

After a week of seeing nothing but water, they were quite shocked to see land ahead. It was a strange feeling when the ship came to a standstill after the constant movement. They docked at Port Said and as Jimmy popped his head through the cabin porthole he had to dodge back quickly as an Egyptian man threw a rope at him. Rowing boats, laden with leather handbags, sandals, sunglasses and all manner of goods for sale, bobbed alongside the ship. Other passengers had caught ropes thrown to them and were viewing the items for sale as they made their way up to them in baskets.

Jimmy and Irene stepped ashore for their very first experience of a foreign land. They were bombarded from the moment their feet touched the sandy road: 'Very good watch Ma'am, very good price Sir'. 'These are very good sunglasses Mrs. Simpson, good for the sun'. The locals called all the men Jack or Charlie and all the ladies Mrs. Simpson as they tried to, somewhat forcefully, entice them into shops. They were offered guided tours, drinks and snacks; anything could be had, for a price. They walked in a group of six, three married couples. The men stood protectively close to their wives as the local men brazenly eyed them up. Little boys and young mothers with babies asked them for money and the Gilly Gilly man performed conjuring tricks. Fresh fish and fruits, covered in flies, were displayed on makeshift stalls, creating an unpleasant smell in the stifling heat. Big old American cars sped by at speed, kicking up dust into their eyes. The English group was pestered and sweaty by the time it returned to the ship, but thrilled and excited by the whole adventure.

It took a while to sail through the Suez Canal. Big liners queued up waiting for their turn and there were many stops as they waited for others to pass. The scenery was mainly sand, with occasional clumps of green growth scattered here and there and the odd building visible in the distance. They passed through a lake in the large town of Ishmalia before entering the Red Sea. The intense heat was way hotter than they had ever imagined, they were completely drained of energy. They found it hard to believe that the next glimpse of land they would catch would be Aden, and not Southampton. But this was not a holiday after all.

Aden was dirty and stifling but they were enchanted to find camels pulling carts and goats wandering about the roads. Again they suffered the onslaught of salesmen offering them anything from *Surf* washing powder to *Leica* cameras. Irene smiled innocently as men offered themselves to her and Jimmy had to explain to her what they were offering themselves for. Her cheeks glowed beetroot red for the entire day. Back on board they cooled down with glasses of ginger beer and got ready for the evening's fancy dress dinner and dance.

With Bombay drawing closer they spent hours filling in custom forms, long drawn out pages full of official questions. They watched their approach into India from the deck. As the magnificent splendour of India's gateway came into sight they felt dizzy with excitement and anticipation. Arrival time was expected to be four o'clock in the afternoon and they were then due to catch the six thirty train for Calcutta. They were delighted when they disembarked almost an hour earlier, allowing extra time to catch the train.

In the customs shed they were asked to write down on a sheet of paper everything they had packed into their trunks. They scoured their memories, trying to remember what they had brought and what they'd decided to leave behind. The officer took his time to read the lists, then opened the trunks and checked every single item. Next, he pointed to Jimmy's crate of books. 'Open it', he demanded. 'What?' Jimmy replied before correcting himself by saying, 'Pardon', in a weak little whimper as he turned pale at the memory of all the nails and screws he'd driven into it. He attempted to explain how difficult it would be to open it and then get it sufficiently sealed again to put on the train. 'Open it'. The officer repeated. But as he circled the box and saw how secure it was he relented, though not before an animated row erupted between all the officers. Instead he insisted that Jimmy write down every book contained in the crate and said he would send someone to check it when they had arrived at their final destination. That was a lucky escape, but by this time it was eight thirty in the evening and they had missed their train and the next one was three days away.

A missionary, stationed in Bombay, was at the docks to greet them and offered them shelter in his home until the next train. Jimmy and Irene accepted his offer with relief and feasted their eyes upon the colourful commotion going on around them. The docks were alive with busyness and noise and they were inundated with offers from thin, barefooted men, to carry and transport their luggage.

On the train, the Howrah Express, they had a carriage with bunk beds to sleep in for the two nights of their journey. They shared it with six people but Irene was the only female among them. On the first night she lay on her bunk, fully clothed and trembling. She squeezed her eyes tightly shut, in a futile attempt to stop the tears that spilled onto her cheeks as she stared at the roof of the train. She concentrated her mind on her sister Doris, who was due to give birth to her first child any day now. Putting her handkerchief over her nose and mouth she quelled her revulsion as the men below, strangers to her, farted and made disgusting sounds clearing their throats. She didn't want to know where they spat. She prayed.

The train was hot and dusty and spewed smoke into the carriages as it passed through jungles and villages where children waved excitedly as they passed. The scenery along the way was enthralling. They'd been told that India looked beautiful at this time of year following the rains, and they were not disappointed.

As they arrived, dusty and hungry, Calcutta greeted them with a buzz of noise and colour. After settling into the room in Sudder Street where they were to spend a few days with the minister of the Christian Church and his wife, getting to know their way around, they went out onto the streets. It was a holiday, and time for the autumn festival of Durga Puja; Hindus were out in their thousands to celebrate. Calcutta was alive with joy as people worshipped the Goddess Durga, the Mother Goddess. Jimmy and Irene walked for miles around the city with their hosts, watching the images of the goddess being carried high. It was a warm evening and main roads and back alleys were alight with a blaze of fireworks in the sky. People danced and sang. The air was heavy with incense, the atmosphere alight with delight. The English couple were enchanted and happy.

The next morning they walked along Sudder Street and onto the Chowringhee Road to buy some provisions they'd need once they arrived at the house in Barrackpore. Jimmy and Irene didn't say much to each other as they took in their first sight of the city in the light of day. The festival was over and the city had resumed its normal routines. Their faces took on a pinched expression as they witnessed families living in huddles on the side streets. Their 'homes' were salvaged plastic and cardboard sheets tied primitively to bamboo canes. Irene didn't let on her horror as she walked among filth, with barefoot children and flea-ridden pi dogs at her heels. Jimmy didn't look into her eyes as boys pawed at him with pleading looks in their eyes. This was reality for them now, and they were going to have to adjust to it quickly.

They caught a train to Barrackpore, just outside Calcutta, and from the station a taxi took them to number six Riverside Road, their new home. The house looked very grand and inviting as they pulled up outside. It was a low, white painted bungalow with green wooden shutters at the windows. A portico provided an imposing welcome and a small lake, surrounded by trees, glistened in the sunshine a short distance away. Jimmy opened the front double doors into the living room and closed them again quickly before Irene could see. Inside, the house, that had stood empty for some time, was thick with dust. It took them five days to scrub the place clean and evict the rats to make it habitable. But once they'd unpacked and added a few homely touches and photographs, they thought it looked lovely. They didn't even mind the little tic-ticky lizards that ran along the walls, and across the picture of Durham Cathedral.

The view from the back of the house was beautiful. From the veranda, where they took breakfast, the garden stretched way, way down to the edge of the River Hooghly, one of the channels through which the sacred water of the Ganges flows into the Bay of Bengal. At full moon a big tidal wave sweeps up it, making a terrific roar as it comes. Jimmy liked to climb onto the roof of the bungalow to watch; it reminded him of home and the sea at Blackhall Rocks.

As Irene sat at her desk, writing a letter home to her family, she saw some baby monkeys at the bottom of the garden. 'Oh you sweet little things', she cooed, as she ran out of the house to greet them. 'Come on', she called, 'come here and let me see you'. Suddenly the baby's mother leapt from a tree and hissed at her aggressively, baring her teeth in a vicious snarl. Irene turned and ran like the wind back into the house and shut the door.

Barrackpore is a village, no bigger than Blackhall. It's a cantonment area, hence its name, an old military and administrative centre that was once under British rule. Jimmy and Irene came into contact with British Army officers and majors who lived nearby. Jimmy occasionally preached, or took funeral services of Ghurkhas in the church at the base. He was responsible for the members of the small, white painted Methodist church in Barrackpore but the majority of his outreach work was in the neighbouring villages and slums of Calcutta.

His first experience of slum dwelling brought a revelation that shocked him to the core of his being. He walked into a narrow street of one such area to talk with people and found living conditions that were beyond his belief. The scene before him was surely conjured from a nightmare. Homes lined either side of streets, made up of corrugated iron sheeting and cardboard, fastened crudely together. The very first home he visited was that of a Christian family and it nearly broke his heart. A grandmother, grandfather, mother, father and their two children lived in one 'room' about seven feet square. The women prepared food on a wooden trestle built up of scrap, and cooked in the doorway on a small, single-ringed cooker fuelled by dried cow dung. The toilet was the open gutter running down the centre of the street, and served everyone. He feared he was going to be sick, both from the stench rising from the gutter and the horror he felt in his soul. The people he sat with were full of warmth and welcomed him with wide smiles and open arms. He received the same, hospitable, treatment in each home he visited in the slum. It was dark as he left in the evening. He got into his battered car, parked on the outskirts, and turned on the headlights to reveal bodies squatting over the gutter, washing their bottoms from water held in tin cans that caught the headlight's glare. He sat in the car feeling stunned.

It was only a matter of weeks before Irene caught her first bout of bacillary dysentery, and Jimmy, gastric 'flu. They'd been so careful with the water they drank, boiling it rapidly, but still the vicious little germs found their way into their systems. As their first Christmas approached they felt thin and debilitated, but the sight of all the cute children in the village had them planning a party for them on Christmas Eve. Irene instructed Ram Smudge, a local man they'd taken on as their cook, on what to make for the children to eat. They'd felt awkward at first, hiring men to work as servants, but it was the way things worked in India and the men needed the incomes. The gardener was a gem with green fingers; he grew chrysanthemums worthy of a prize at Chelsea. Rintu, the young boy hired to sweep up in the house, knew every trick in the book when it came to skiving, but when he was invited to the party he swept with a vengeance. The local children had a wonderful time playing games and eating more food than they'd seen in a long time. Ram Smudge walked into the garden, with a big smile on his face, carrying a large tray. 'Look Misses Irene, please, your lemon meringue pie, just how you told me', he said to Irene as his eyes burst with pride. 'Oh that's perfect', she told him, and clapped her hands in delight at the fluorescent pink mound on the tray.

Titagarh is the next village along from Barrackpore. Within its boundary lived a colony of shunted and rejected people. Their only crime was to have had the rotten misfortune to have caught the dreaded disease known as leprosy. Some had been banished from their homes and families, chased from their villages in fear. People didn't want the lepers, with their unsightly disfigurements and deformities, anywhere near them.

Leprosy, though not strictly fatal, deals a cruel blow to the humanity of men, women and children. Caused by a bacillus, *Mycobacterium Lepra*, the disease is not highly infectious, contrary to popular belief, and most people carry a natural immunity. But in poverty-stricken areas, such as those in India, it seeks its many victims. When Praem Chand first discovered the patch, pale against his naturally dark skin, he felt a sickening fear in the pit of his stomach. He felt no sensation when he touched it with his finger. He kept it covered so that no-one would see. More patches appeared and gradually the feeling in his fingers and toes lessened. He knew his labouring days in the factory were numbered. People began to notice and recoiled in horror. They were afraid to be near him. Over time ugly lumps appeared on his face and nobody touched him any more, not even his wife and children.

He had to leave his home, the crude shelter in the slum. He took to sitting outside the station at Howrah, holding out his hand, in shame, but dependent on offerings from passersby. No-one looked anymore into his kind and unusually blue eyes. He'd never worn shoes on his feet so the skin had become tough. But now he couldn't feel them, and if he stood on a sharp stone he didn't know it, until it bled. Sores appeared on their surface and began to develop into ulcers, oozing yellow puss. He listened to conversations taking place around him and learned of places where others, like him, lived. He knew that it was intended he should hear these things. He knew he was not wanted. He left his little spot outside the station.

Jimmy and Irene first went to Titagarh with a small group of Christians from the church in Barrackpore within a few weeks of their arrival in India. They entered the compound of outcasts, with their permission, and Jimmy led a short service in the courtyard. They sang hymns and said prayers. The lepers came out of their cramped hovels to listen and join in the singing. Irene had nursed patients with amputated limbs back home in England, but here she looked at people whose fingers, toes and noses had been eaten away by infection. Those with only sore, ulcerated stumps for feet and hands crawled along the ground. What a shocking sight and yet, this crowd were the most cheerful bunch that Jimmy and Irene had met so far. At the end of the service Jimmy said the Benediction. When all was silent, Praem Chand threw his hands in the air and turned his noseless face to the sky and shouted, 'Praise to Jesus'. The visiting group were stunned at first, but joined in, laughing, with the chorus as the whole compound yelled at the top of their voices, 'Praise to Jesus'. A humble Jimmy and Irene wondered just who, in fact, was really delivering God's message of love.

TEARS AND PAIN

Jimmy was charged with zeal. He threw himself into the discovery of his new surroundings. He'd never seen so many people in one place before, not even at a football match. The people were all so different, their lifestyles and culture fascinated him. No amount of training in college could really paint the picture of such a vibrant, colourful, energetically crowded place. Thousands and thousands of people filled the streets. Following the partition of east from west Bengal, refugees had flooded into Calcutta from what was known as East Pakistan, now Bangladesh, but with nowhere for them to live many lay on the streets, homeless and hungry. Calcutta was not geared towards such a vast number of people, the roads were not adequate, nor the drainage system to cater for so huge an influx. Poverty and disease were rife.

He'd come out to India filled with a burning passion for God that he intended to shower over its people. He was full of energy, enthusiasm and love for humankind. He'd been appointed to the Mills Area Mission to offer help and support in the running of the church. The long term aim was to bring about unity in the Christian sector and to amalgamate the Methodist, Anglican and Baptist denominations into one body. His vision was one of packed churches praising God and reaching out to help an impoverished community. It was not long before reality dawned in the frame of a very different picture. He found himself in the midst of a circuit full of problems. Accounts had not been kept so there were none ready for audit, matters of administration needed urgent attention, properties screamed out for maintenance. The small congregations were somewhat apathetic. His priorities, it appeared, were already set for him. His heart yearned to get stuck into the work he'd believed he'd come here to do, but instead he found himself submerged in ledgers and book-keeping for the self-funding church he was in charge of. When one of his native colleagues confronted him with the question, 'Why have you come here?' followed by the statement, 'We don't need you', Jimmy almost asked himself the same question. But the missionaries were still being invited to come, as guests, and help to run the Christian churches. Jimmy wanted them to get to the point where they did indeed no longer require help.

The circuit they were in was the only Hindi speaking one around the area of Calcutta, the others spoke colloquial Bengali. Jimmy and Irene's limited knowledge of the language was a hindrance and people spoke much more quickly than the teachers had back in the language classes in England. Just as Irene discovered that she was expecting their first child they were sent, as expected, by the Missionary Society, to a language school in the hills for a few months. They felt that if they could really master their understanding and use of the Hindi language they would find it easier to pick up and grasp Bengali by living amongst the locals.

They set off on an exhausting three day journey, taking a

bus, a train, and a ferry across the sacred water of the Ganges, another train and finally a taxi from Dehra Doon. The car wove its way, zigzagging seven thousand five hundred feet high up the mountain road, skirting around hair-raising bends with death threatening sheer drops. The views were breathtaking, like a snow covered fairyland but the air grew increasingly cooler the higher they rose. When the taxi stopped, four miles short of their destination, the freezing cold air caught their throats and made them gasp. The final stint of the journey had to be made by foot and a group of coolies were on hand to help them. Irene was put into a chair tied to poles and lifted from the ground as the men raised the poles onto their thin shoulders. Fortunately for them she was still a featherweight. Jimmy refused his chair and chose to walk and help the poor thin chaps with no shoes on their feet with the abundant piles of luggage. Their new temporary home was a boarding house in the hills of Landour, and the nearest shop was an hour's walk back down the hill in Mussoorie. They were pleased that their food was going to be provided for them during their stay.

Study, alongside other missionaries who were all American, was intense. Classes took place from Monday to Friday, with tests set at the end of every week. Jimmy began to feel as though he was swimming in treacle, and would never be free from the burden of exams. Nothing much happened in the mountains and the only light relief came from the wireless they had the use of. It was a treat indeed to sit back on a Friday evening and listen to an English play followed by, for Jimmy, the football results. Occasionally, on a Saturday, he managed to tune into a Sunderland match and forget everything as he paced the floor and punched the air with joy when they scored a goal.

The mountain air was invigorating, but their health

began to suffer from a deprivation of vitamins in the food they were offered. What milk they had was watered down and had to be boiled until it contained little nourishment. One Saturday morning they walked to the shop to clear their heads and found some bottles of *Metatone* tonic on a shelf. Jimmy's Mam swore by the goodness contained in the syrup and always took a drop when she felt rundown. Jimmy pounced on the bottle and felt his vitality spring back into action before he'd even unscrewed the lid.

When the Principal of the language college asked Jimmy for his assistance in protecting the few cows belonging to the local herdsmen, he obliged. A panther had been prowling around at night and had killed a cow. Jimmy was given a rifle and told to dress up warmly. They set off, after dark, and trekked into the hills to set up camp for the night within sight of the dead cow. A panther will keep coming back to its catch to feed from it, Jimmy was told. Their job was to shoot it when it returned. They settled down, looking like a couple of Michelin men, in the many layers of clothes they wore against the bitter cold of night. The panther crept, stealthily, towards the dead animal, its eyes shining like jewels in the dark. The men couldn't get a clear aim so it got the better of their bullets. They sat and watched till it returned for another feed, teasing them with its agility as it slunk close to the ground and wove through trees and bushes. It circled them throughout the night, but got away free, with its belly full. Happily, not full of them.

By the time the summer weather had warmed them, and they were able to hold fluent conversations in Hindi they were keen to get back to Barrackpore to proceed with their work. They'd passed oral exams and had no more to face until September when they would sit three days of written examinations in Calcutta. When the time came for them to leave Landour, Jimmy was determined to find an easier way to transport the heavy cases down the four mile trek to the waiting taxi. Irene put all their clothes on coat hangers and Jimmy hung them onto a walking stick he'd bought as a souvenir. He slung the stick across his shoulder and walked down the mountain with them swinging rhythmically behind him.

They arrived home to Riverside Road, dirty, smelly and dusty from the train. Their bearer, Ram Smudge, had looked after the house well in their absence and greeted them with a big smile, showing the gaps between his rotten teeth. In honour of their safe return he'd even changed into a clean shirt. He didn't see the point in changing his shirt and dhoti every day when after only an hour or so they were already damp with sweat. Irene had pestered Jimmy to gently point out to him that sweat accumulated over a week was not as sweetly acceptable as the sweat of one day. Perhaps, at last, she thought, he's getting the point.

Sadly the church had not fared so well over the months. The accounts Jimmy had struggled to set up had not been kept up. He frowned in despair at the thought of yet more long hours to be filled with the task of administration. In his absence it had been decided that Jimmy must take over as superintendent of the circuit, a position he had not anticipated so early on in his ministry but one he was prepared to accept. It seemed that he was needed after all, if only to pour oil on the troubled waters of congregational squabbles brewed from a lack of organisation and direction. What he really wanted was to bring the people together and focus their minds on the vast social welfare problem manifesting itself all around them.

The church in Titagarh was nothing more than a scruffy little shop in a bazaar. It had no lighting other than a candle. Jimmy was just beginning to feel comfortable and confident preaching in Hindi but he struggled to read his notes and Bible passages under the flicker of a flame. He took his tool box with him to the weekly prayer meeting. At the end, quite some time later, for the Indian Christians liked to pray, he set to work fixing up a light. He extended cables and brought the crude electricity supply into the room. This created a huge audience, attracting shoppers and passersby from the bazaar. They were all fascinated to watch the 'sahib' working with his hands, a job not normally associated with English missionaries. All eyes were upon him as he hammered nails and tacks into the walls to secure the cable. The people watched intently, their bodies leaning to the right and left to keep the hammer in view. Each time the hammer missed a nail they sucked in their breath and chorused 'Aray Baap', 'Oh Father'. Jimmy asked them to stand back as he flicked on the switch and they all clapped excitedly as he pronounced, 'We have light'.

He was invited to sit with some of the curious onlookers and partake of a cup of chai. Jim was eager to mix with members of the community outside the environment of the church, people he now lived alongside, and this small opportunity thrilled him. He spent time in the bazaar listening carefully to men talking about their Hindu faith and the gods they worshipped and trusted. It was a privilege to be in such company and he was overjoyed with the outcome of the afternoon. Finding a way to infiltrate into communities was not easy; trust had to be earned when interacting with people of different faiths. He was the foreigner here. He was the one with the different coloured skin. Often, as he walked the streets, he would be followed by young children who imitated him, giggling. When he turned around to smile at them they ran away, screaming. He'd overheard mothers disciplining their offspring by threatening to call the white man if they didn't behave. The invitation to share time this afternoon had proved to be a valuable interaction and touched him deeply.

He was learning more about himself and his mission daily. He realised that he wasn't simply here to convert everybody to Christianity, but to share, really share faiths with others. His path to God was through Jesus Christ, for Hindus it was many gods that led them to a supreme being, for Muslims it was Muhammad. They were all on their respective journeys. He felt it wasn't for him to push and probe and inflict his views onto people who were quite happy and content with their beliefs, he was here to share in their sufferings and their joys.

He burst into the bungalow ready to expound his experience onto his wife, but instead found her pacing the floor with her hands on her swollen belly. Her waters had broken, she told him, but she felt no pain whatsoever. He put her in the car and drove to the post office, as one might in such a case. With no telephone in the house they had to use the community one available at the post office.

Irene talked to the minister's wife in Calcutta and was relieved to hear that their mutual friend, wife of another missionary and close friend of Jimmy's, was staying there. 'Come straight here', she was told. When they arrived the house in Sudder Street was in a commotion. The two women were rushing around in preparation and floodlights had been set up in a bedroom. A lady doctor was on hand and Joyce, Irene's friend and a midwife, set about examining her and said the baby would be coming shortly. 'But I've felt no pain at all', laughed Irene. She'd had an operation on her spine before she and Jimmy were married and apparently the nerves in her uterus lacked any sensitivity. The only pain she suffered was during the last half hour before Timu, a healthy baby boy, popped into the world on the fifth of October 1955.

Irene was ecstatic to be a Mum at last. To hold their very own baby in her arms was a dream she thought she'd never fulfil during the long years of waiting to be married. Timu was a healthy, bouncing treasure they adored. Jimmy sent telegrams home to England to announce the birth with great pride and immediately set to taking photographs.

Shortly after the birth Jimmy began to feel quite poorly. He got one sore throat after another and his body temperature fluctuated daily. A doctor diagnosed a bout of laryngitis and pharyngitis and prescribed medications that cost them a great deal of money. Over the next few months he got constant stomach aches and vomited after every bit of food he ate. One Sunday morning in February, as he was taking a service in the church at Kankinara, he collapsed into unconsciousness. He knew nothing about the episode at all until he came round an hour later at home. A doctor was sent for and told him that he'd had a fit. He had to confess that he'd had a similar occurrence while they were in Landour. That time it happened when he was asleep and only Irene saw it. Jimmy was deeply embarrassed that it had happened in public and couldn't imagine how awful he must have looked as lay on the floor of the church, shaking and foaming at the mouth.

The doctor had Jimmy sent to a nursing home in Calcutta for tests. While he was there he had severe pains in his chest as well. The tests revealed that he had an infection in his stomach and pleurisy in his lungs. 'Have you eaten any pork recently?' he was asked. 'Yes, we had a lot of it in the boarding house at language school in the hills', Jimmy replied. The outcome of many tests, including an encephalogram, proved that the convulsions were probably not caused by epilepsy as such. Jimmy had got tape-worms from the pork he'd eaten, and although he didn't fully understand the diagnosis, the long and short of it was that one of the little tinkers had wiggled its way into his brain and caused him to black out and convulse. 'Well can you get them out?' he asked, filled with horror at the thought of slimy little worms taking over his body. 'No', the doctor replied, 'we'll give you some medication that will kill them'. The tablets he took had Jimmy begging his good Lord for death, or at least mercy. His entire body was gripped in a vice of pain and sickness. Poor Irene was worried almost beyond endurance as she tried to bring him some comfort.

Jimmy was ordered to take some time to rest. He was severely weak and had no energy; the weight had dropped from his lean frame until his cheekbones and ribs protruded from beneath his sallow skin. He spent his time playing with Timu and pottering in their beautiful garden filled with dahlias, pansies, sweet peas and exotic fruit trees. Of course he could no longer drive in case he had another fit, but he didn't want the car anyway, the money spent on the car could, he felt, be put to better use in the circuit and travelling in buses allowed him greater opportunity to mingle. With unexpected free time on his hands he made a photographic enlarger out of tin cans and scraps that he'd collected in case they came in useful. Pictures of the baby could now be blown up and sent to the family in England. May and Ernie, the proud aunties and uncles, drooled over the photographs they received and sent gifts for the newborn. Lizzie said that Timu was a bonny baby, 'but eee Jimmy you're looking thin, are you alright over there?'

As soon as his health permitted he began to put his concerns for the lepers into action. There were thousands of leprosy sufferers in Titagarh that, so far, no-one had offered to help. The plight of the folk in the colony, cheerful souls despite their sorrowful state, had filled Jimmy and Irene's hearts with tenderness. Jimmy's passion was to set up a clinic to serve them, offering help, advice and much needed treatment. He knew of three such clinics in Calcutta but that was too far away for the people who could not get a ride on a bus because of the nature of the disease and the stigma attached to it. Jimmy visited the clinics to talk with the doctors and they agreed to give their help for one day a week to get him started. He began a laborious project to acquire funding and suitable land on which to build the clinic. Meetings with council officials left him frustrated and had him gripping every ounce of his patience with both hands. Added to that, nobody wanted the lepers anywhere near their homes. It was going to be a long and hard process but he had the wheels in motion. In the meantime Jimmy continued to visit the colony regularly and organised regular milk and rice supplies. He began to get to know the people well and never ceased to marvel at the delight they showed just to see his face among them, or when he simply held their hands.

*

They'd been in India for two years when Jimmy returned to their home one day bone weary and troubled. Timu, a happy, healthy and tubby baby was almost one year old. He held his arms out to his Daddy and chortled gleefully when tickled and cuddled. Daddy had just taken the funeral of a six-year-old girl. Her family were poor and lived in one of the thousands of dwellings that sit on row upon row in a slum. Sindhu, the little girl, had had a tummy upset for two weeks but her parents did not have enough money to pay for the medication that would have made her well again. After the funeral Jimmy waded through the flooded streets, awash with faeces and drowned vermin, remnants of the devastation caused by a cyclone that had just recently hit the Bay of Bengal. Many homes were in ruins, families were bereft and goats and cows roamed about, pitifully, looking for food and water. Jimmy kissed Timu's warm, plump cheek and held out an arm to Irene. Their home had been spared from ruin, only the interior walls were damp. He held his family close to him before turning back out onto the streets to offer what help he could.

It was the rainy season which added extra trauma to the already futile attempts at clearing roads. After working in the pit Jimmy was not afraid of hard, dirty, physical work and willingly joined men in clearing away debris that cluttered the village. The air was hot and sticky, the heat sickening, combined with the rancid stench from overflowing drains. When Jimmy heard the screeching of brakes, a thud and a stomach-churning squeal he vomited. Their little puppy, given to them by Rintu, the sweeper boy, lay lifeless on the road. Jimmy ran to his little dog and picked him up in his arms with tears streaming down his face. Jip must have run after him as he left the house. He carried him, tenderly, back home and saw Irene calling the puppy from the front veranda. Her face crumpled when she saw the fluffy black and white bundle in Jimmy's arms. 'Oh no', she wailed, 'I couldn't stop him; he flew out of the door after you'. Blume, their gentle Alsatian dog, whimpered and came to lick Jip's wounds to no avail.

It had been a thoroughly exhausting day and Jim felt useless in the face of the many catastrophes that seemed to surround him. The tragic death of the little girl who could have lived with the aid of a few doses of medication saddened him deeply, as did the future of the people in the villages who'd lost their homes and worldly possessions. Jimmy sat down on the veranda late in the evening; his body was aching from head to foot. A letter had arrived that day from his Mam and he opened it with an expectant smile on his face. Her news and gossip lulled him into a state of cheer, turning his mind, briefly, from the devastation outside his front door. Irene heard his sudden, infectious laughter and asked to be let in on the joke, 'Jimmy', he read his Mother's familiar handwriting from the thin blue sheet of airmail, 'do you know where I put the guarantee card for my Hoover? It's making a funny noise'.

As they lay in bed that night, feeling sad and exhausted, they heard a noise in the back garden. Jimmy leapt out of bed to open the shutter. Three men were carrying their wicker furniture off the veranda. One was already close to the bottom of the long garden. Blume started to bark furiously and jump up at the glass doors in an attempt to see the robbers off.

'Where's the key?' he yelled. 'Ram Smudge, where's the key to the door?' Ram Smudge scuttled from room to room, opening drawers and cupboards as he scratched his head in confusion.

'Ah', the bearer proclaimed.

'Have you found it, good man, bring it quickly', Jimmy called.

'No Reverend Jim, I don't know where I've put the key but I've found the post you were looking for last week'.

Jimmy and Irene could only laugh as they stood and watched the three men pack their furniture into a rowing boat parked on the river Hooghly, and sail off into the night. Blume went back to her bed and tried to sleep without the comfort of her little friend Jip. Irene snuggled up to Jimmy and asked,

'Is this a good time to tell you that I'm expecting again?'

'Oh, my lovely Irene, it is indeed. That's the best news I've heard all day', he answered as he pulled her to him.

Jimmy, carrying Timu, stepped off the bus and helped Irene down the steps. They all heaved a sigh of relief for the bus had been full to capacity and way beyond, with passengers hanging onto the outside and sitting on the roof.

'It reminds me of being in the cage at Blackhall pit', he said, with a smile on his face at the recollection.

'But this is a far cry from Middle Street', Irene commented as they made their way into the hustle and bustle of Newmarket to get some fresh bread and cakes from the Jewish bakery. Timu, now eighteen months old, loved the round pink fairy cakes that could only be bought there. Irene, heavily pregnant, had a craving for some freshly baked bread with butter spread thickly on top. They'd decided to combine the shopping trip with a doctor's appointment to check on the baby and Irene's general health.

They bought yards of cotton material in the market for Irene to make dresses for herself, shirts for Jim (gradually Jimmy's name had been shortened to Jim like his father before him) and shorts for Timu. They'd brought a Singer sewing machine with them from England. It had been a manual one, operated by a small wheel with a handle that had to be turned. But Jim had been given a broken sewing machine motor from one of the majors at the barracks. Nobody that knew Jim threw anything away before first asking him if he wanted it. Sure enough, Jim, ever resourceful, repaired the motor and attached it to Irene's sewing machine so that it now worked as well as any electric one.

Back at Riverside Road they discovered Ram Smudge and Rintu on the roof of the bungalow jumping up and down in frenzy. Howls, barks and yelps echoed from the living room. Jim ushered Irene and Timu into their Indian friend's house next-door before going to investigate. Armed with a sturdy stick he came face to face with a rabid dog. Blume was fighting the dog and trying to get it out of the house, her nose gushed with blood from its vicious bite. Together in battle, man and his dog managed to get the mad dog outside where Irene and her friends had alerted some soldiers who were on hand to shoot it. Jim reached up to the high shelf, out of Timu's reach, to retrieve the emergency medical supply to tend to Blume's nose. As he picked the metal box up a rat, the size of a rabbit, hissed and stared him right in the eye before lunging, open mouthed, towards his face. Jim shot his face to the side but not before the rat sunk its teeth into his right shoulder. Man and dog, shocked and shaking, allowed themselves to be taken to the doctor and vet, respectively. They both yelled when the long, thick, shiny needles jabbed into their backsides.

Work was busy for Jim. Irene helped him on the administration side by attending to all the filing, but with a toddler and new baby on the way she had her hands full. By now Jim was running the circuit of five churches alone without the support of another minister. On Sundays he left home at seven forty-five to take the first service of the day. From there he travelled twelve miles to the next church for the second, then thirty miles to the third, and fourteen miles back for the fourth. Their friends in Calcutta, the minister and his wife they stayed with when they first arrived, had returned to England. The missionary had suffered a brutal encounter on a train to Darjeeling. He'd fallen asleep on the long journey and muggers dealt him a blow to the head, robbed him and threw him from the train, leaving him for dead. Thankfully he survived, but only just. With severe injuries to his face and body, and a cracked skull, he lay unconscious for seven hours until he was rescued.

Frustrations abounded for Jim in the churches. He had many ideas for the circuit and many visions for growth, outreach, as well as the hoped for merging of denominations. But he was faced with a lack of enthusiasm wherever he turned. He could have stormed his way through and implemented changes at his own discretion, but that was not the way he liked to work. He was not prepared to do anything unless he could take the people along with him. It must be a joint venture. It was their church after all, he was just the guest, and they would all still be there long after he'd moved on. They had to want to move forward, sideways or backwards, he was not prepared to drag them kicking and screaming. He didn't want them to feel resentful; he wanted them to feel joyful. 'Therefore, we must go along step by step together', he said encouragingly at the leaders' meeting, to which all members agreed wholeheartedly as they applauded him, then returned their attention, yet again, to the idea of a new church organ.

In a letter that Jim sent home to the family in England he wrote: *'It is a long and painful road and on the face of it, it may appear that I am being lazy and doing nothing, or I should say achieving nothing. There is plenty to do here. I love these people dearly but I struggle to understand their minds. I think if I stay here for the rest of my life I will still not understand the Indian mind. I believe the missionary has not much longer in India, and this is not for political reasons. It is because we are coming to a point in the life of the Church in India when the missionary is more of a hindrance than an asset to the progress of the Church. When a child grows into adult life the parents must let him think and choose for him or herself, though being ready with encouragement, guidance and love. Here we are trying to do the thinking for the Indian Church and, I feel, it is hindering development. It is a big problem. We younger missionaries feel it more than the older ones. The Indians don't really want us now. I will stay on until 1960 unless something happens to prevent it. But I doubt if I will be returning after my first furlough. I don't want to speak too early, of course. It all depends on God's guidance and the need of the day'.*

Jim was fully behind the idea of Church union. The aim was to create one Church under the title of 'The Church of North India', and it was hoped to be set up and running by 1961. He was on a train, travelling home from synod wearing his full clerical gear. A Hindu man came to sit next to him and asked him to explain the different kinds of Christianity. The train journey was too long to skip the question and the man was very inquisitive. Jim explained that Christianity is the religion of the Methodists, Anglicans, Baptists and Catholics alike. He explained the different concepts behind each denomination and the varying forms of worship. But the man, though intelligent and well educated, could not grasp the idea. He was perplexed; he leaned forward with a frown on his face as he tried to get his head round it all. Jim felt great pain and sadness in his heart when the man said in his confusion, 'You are telling me that Christianity is love, fellowship together with Christ, and forgiveness. Then why are you all separate?'

Why indeed, thought Jim. How do you explain something which, after all, is only the work of man and not of God? It sounds as though we're saying one thing with one breath then denying it with the other. He did not feel very proud.

Jim was longing to see Irene and Timu after the week-long separation of synod. But their evening together was not restful. A Muslim man came to the house and told Jim that he wanted to convert to Christianity. 'So where will you put me when my family and friends disown me for leaving my faith?' he asked. The poor man was so desperate to find work that he would have sold his soul for a job and he thought that Jim could provide one if he converted. After a long discussion, in which Jim explained that this was not how it worked, and that it was important to be true to one's faith, he went to bed with a very heavy heart.

As well as searching for land for a clinic, Jim was also searching for land for the site of a new church building. He felt at times as though life was just one long series of property planning meetings. He was either selling land belonging to the circuit or buying new land for a new project. He'd been granted permission to drive again by the doctors and had bought a second-hand motor bike which he'd repaired and done up. Driving back from the viewing of a piece of land, his thrill of being at one with the elements astride his machine was interrupted. The put-putting sound of his little old bike was being drowned out by a fleet of manly riders, about to show off, mockingly, on their mean machines. He grinned to himself and patted his handlebar affectionately. But the grin vanished from his face as the motorcyclists surrounded him and forced him into a disused warehouse. Little Jimmy looked small fry encircled by the menacing tormentors who, one by one, got off their bikes and walked slowly, but determinedly, towards him bearing knives and truncheons. Two of the thugs picked him up and backed him against a wall, pinning him with their hands around his throat. He felt a searing pain as a truncheon bludgeoned into his left side and again as a fist struck a blow to his right cheekbone. He saw his own blood on the fist of his attacker and caught the shimmer of steel on the blade of a knife that was held just a little bit too close for comfort.

Jim had the gift of the gab; often it came in handy, other times it did not. The land that he was interested in belonged, unofficially, to this group of gentlemen, it appeared. They had their mark on it and were making the point that it was, most definitely, not for sale or rent. Jim found his voice and said, 'OK but I can see you are men of reason, let's talk about this'. He proceeded to praise them on the power of their motorbikes. He commented on the thumping engine beat of their *Royal Enfield Bullet 350's,* he laughed as he compared the roar they made, to the meow of his little put-put. He told the gang that his dream machine, back in England, was the Harley Davidson, but that he doubted he would ever be able to afford one. And so a discussion took place about makes and models of two-wheeled machines. The thugs, drawn quite out of context from the situation at hand, were baffled into submission. The outcome was that Jim would not be looking to buy the land, and they would not be piercing his skin with the blades of their knives. His gift of the gab had served him well and he offered his hand in a shake of friendship as they parted to allow him to leave. Jim rode home and wobbled into the bungalow on legs like a bendy doll, his arms flailing about as he fell prostrate at Irene's feet.

Shortly after the event that had Jim grimacing with pain every time he moved, Irene went into labour a few weeks earlier than expected. This time she did feel pain from contractions that started at four o'clock in the afternoon. Jim was visiting in Calcutta and had to be contacted by the Indian friends next-door. He ran into the house at six o'clock and was alarmed to see Irene in so much pain; they both realised that it was too late to travel into the hospital in Calcutta. It was all happening very quickly. Jim jumped onto his motorbike and sped to the post office telephone and spoke to one of his English colleagues whose wife was a retired doctor but no longer practising. They came to the rescue, arriving at eight o'clock in the evening. An hour before midnight it became obvious that something was very wrong, it was a breech birth and they had no equipment to deal with it. A doctor was needed for the delivery urgently. A local female doctor arrived and a great deal of shouting and controversy took place; the doctor's breath carried the unmistakable smell of liquor. She was not acting in a competent manner and showed little regard for the wellbeing of Irene, who was delirious with pain, or the baby. At twelve forty-five twin boys were born. Their bodies were lifeless, neither one of them drew breath. They were dead.

It was a night of horror. Before leaving, with her payment, the local doctor suggested that she put the bodies in the river. Jim steered her out of the house sharply and shut the door forcibly behind her. But something did have to be done with the bodies. He tenderly wrapped the perfectly formed babies in a sheet. He made a simple coffin from wood and laid his boys gently, snuggled together, inside. In the early morning darkness, just before dawn, Jim rolled up his sleeves and dug a grave right at the bottom of the garden on the riverbank. With his bare hands he moved the earth and lowered the tiny coffin into the hole and covered it with mud. He formed the silent words in his mind: 'Forasmuch as these children are in the care of the Almighty God, we therefore commit their bodies to the ground, earth to earth, ashes to ashes, dust to dust, in sure and certain hope of eternal life, through our Lord Jesus Christ. Amen'.

Irene lay on her bed, staring at the ceiling, feeling an

overwhelming sense of emptiness inside her. Jim sat at the base of a tree, his gaze resting on the water as it rippled and lapped against the muddy bank and watched the sun rise over the River Hooghly, bringing with it another new day.

END OF AN ERA

The summer of the twins was a tough one for all the inhabitants of Calcutta. Soaring temperatures reached one hundred and eight degrees in the longest hot spell known in Bengal for many years. Epidemics of cholera, smallpox and influenza swept through the city and in his diary, Jim described Calcutta as 'a human scrap heap with bodies lying everywhere'.

Food was not good: vegetables, potatoes and rice shrivelled in the extreme heat and meat became too risky to eat. The bungalow in Barrackpore was infested with mice, rats and ants, Irene and Timu got dysentery and Jim caught 'flu, they were all in a sorry state. Burglars again targeted their property and scuttled off with Jim's typewriter and his prize possession, the wireless he'd made himself. With no television to amuse themselves in the evenings and only a limited supply of novels to read, Jim had enrolled in a home study course in radio engineering to occupy his curious mind. The thieves made off with bed linen, towels, postage stamps, money and all Ram Smudge's clothes, even the sweaty shirt he'd worn for a week.

The work at the leper colony continued to fuel Jim's passion. The doctors in Calcutta had kept their word and visited weekly to offer treatment and advice. They dressed ulcerated skin and open sores but of course with no clinic available the lepers still had to walk on newly bandaged feet so the ulcers had little chance to heal. A petite lady, dressed in a white sari with a blue band border, was following her own calling on the streets of Calcutta. Mother Teresa, whose name was unknown to the world at this time, was providing a mobile leprosy clinic service. She and Jim came into contact with one another, each through their own course of work. They joined forces in Titagarh and Mother Teresa brought one of her mobile clinics to a piece of land, finally made available by the Titagarh Municipal Council to serve the lepers that Jim had come to know and love with great affection. Conditions began to improve for the lepers as new drugs became available. Eventually the dream of a permanent clinic became a reality and with regular treatments they felt hope rise in their hearts.

Sadly, before the clinic was fully up and running Jim and Irene's health began to deteriorate further. Irene had an infection following the delivery of the twins and Jim contracted amoebic dysentery. Their bodies grew so weak that they could hardly walk. Jim continued to work until the Missionary Society stepped in and had them and little Timu sent to a hospital in Serenga for urgent treatment. When the doctor stuck what felt to Jim like a lamppost up his backside to take a look inside, his yell echoed off the hospital's walls. The painful examination revealed that his bowels were lined with a mass of ulcers and that tapeworms were still evidently enjoying his body as their home. He had to take more of the vile medication that had him pleading for mercy. They'd been in India for four years and were not due to take a furlough, return trip home, for another two. But the doctor's report insisted that they return to England immediately for rest and recuperation. Jim was distraught at the prospect of leaving his work at such a crucial time, particularly with the lepers, but both his wife and his body were in desperate need of a reprieve.

It was with a troubled heart that he boarded the ship in a homeward direction. The supply of food was in equal abundance to that on their first, outbound sailing, but neither Jim nor Irene could face much of it. The thrill of seeing their families again urged them on, that and the smile on Timu's face as he celebrated his third birthday and blew out the candles on his cake. Then somewhere, between the shores of India and England, I was conceived, but I'd rather not think about that if you don't mind.

Lizzie and May, drawn together by the homecoming, clasped their hands to their mouths in shock when they each saw their child approaching them at the crowded docks. They knew they'd been unwell but the letters had glossed over the extent of their illnesses. Irene had a haunted look about her eyes. Jim's sallow skin had a grey tinge to it and his frame looked skeletal. Timu hid behind his mother and looked confused to see so many white-skinned people in one place.

Jim threw his arms around his mother and held her as if he never again wanted to let her go. Irene fell into her mother's arms and gave herself up to the warmth and comfort of her embrace. The two grandmothers cooed and drooled over little Timu who was not at all sure about all the kissing and cuddling he was expected to return. The doting women were, after all, strangers to him. Jim caught Edwin's eye and the lump that was lodged in his throat rent him speechless as the two men embraced. Edwin, and his father, Bob Bradley, had driven the two mothers in one of their cars all the way to Liverpool to collect the sick and weary travellers. It was a grand welcome, but for Irene tinged with a new sadness. Her father, Ernie Robinson, had not been able to travel to Liverpool. He was not well, but he didn't really understand that he was not well. While his daughter had been away his mind had begun to wander and he'd grown increasingly confused. The diagnosis was Alzheimer's disease. Furlough was to be a bitter sweet respite from the traumas suffered in Bengal.

Perhaps the sweetest part was the warmth and sharing of the family gathering at Christmas shortly after their arrival home. Jim's ears rang with the constant chatter of the women while the men competed in sound level with a flow of banter and laughter. Timu became acquainted with his cousins who were intrigued by both his complexion and his accent. Having been born in Calcutta his skin had naturally darkened from exposure to the sun. On the boat from Bombay Jim and Irene had talked to him only in English and tried to teach him new words but he spoke his native tongue as may a foreigner on vacation. He was shy, reserved and intimidated by the animated crowd that overwhelmed him. His fascination with newly discovered toys and the big square, boxed television, however, captured his attention and held him riveted.

The smell of roasting turkey wafted throughout the house on Tweddle Crescent. Steam from bubbling pans of vegetables, and homemade Christmas pudding misted the windows. Jim and Irene's taste buds were aroused, almost beyond endurance, by the old and familiar smell of traditional fare. Jim knew a moment of sheer ecstasy as he cut his knife into the succulent meat dripping in gravy, and savoured the flavours on his tongue with reverence. His plate was stacked high by his mother who revelled in the precious opportunity to once again feed her only son. Though it grieved her to note that his appetite was diminished after all the stomach problems he'd encountered and not yet recovered from.

After dinner, once all the pots, pans and plates had been washed up, the troupe walked across the cliff tops and made their way to Margaret and Joe's house in the late afternoon. Preparation for the evening's entertainment began. Jim, George and Charlie (Joe was a little more reserved) dressed up in shawls, aprons and headscarves and put bright red lipstick on their lips and cheeks. They paraded into the parlour causing the women to erupt with laughter, as they sang a song by the Beverley Sisters: *'Sugar in the morning, sugar in the evening....'* Everybody took a turn on the 'stage' with poems, recitals, songs or a comedy act. The women busied themselves with food preparation as an open sing-song continued. The children, all boys, loved every minute of it. When all were replete and could not imagine ever eating again a hush fell over the crowded room. Joe's father, Grandad Hewson, a quiet and gentle man, stood with his back towards the fire and took his pipe out of his mouth. He sang, melodiously, *'Good night Irene, Irene, goodnight Irene....'* and all the women in the house sniffed and wiped their eyes at his tenderness, particularly Irene. A beautiful and poignant day had been had by all.

On Boxing Day the Robinsons had a get-together. May and Ernie had spent Christmas day with Doris, Irene's elder sister and her husband Jim in a less rowdy environment. Ronnie, the little brother, now home from the navy, caught up on old times and spent hours playing with the children. Ernie enjoyed the childish games but most of the time he was in a world of his own. The two expectant sisters exchanged notes on pregnancy and childcare and shared their excitement about Ronnie's imminent marriage to his beautiful fiancée Evelyn. The girls were happy and content to be together with their Mum. After another huge meal of cold turkey, bubble and squeak with pickled onions and piccalilli, Ernie picked up his plate, full of uneaten food, and put it upside down on his head. He laughed at his antics and the three little boys, watching in fascination, put their hands to their plates, eager to copy him. Their mothers intervened but the adults could not help but join with Ernie in his merriment. In his childlike frame of mind he was enjoying himself. May's laughter turned to tears as she disappeared into the back yard.

Winter blossomed into spring and spring into summer. Irene and Jim were on the beach at Blackhall Rocks with Timu when Irene felt the familiar contractions grip her belly. In a moment of panic she tugged Jim's arm with a trace of fear in her eyes. 'It's alright pet', he reassured her, 'come on, we'll go straight to hospital'. They went to Tweddle Crescent to collect her things. Margaret was there with Lizzie and took charge of Timu. Timu did not object; he'd learned quickly that fun and oodles of love went hand in hand with all the Aunties. 'Now make sure you come home with a baby girl Irene', she called as they left the house. At ten minutes past three on the following morning, after a normal, uneventful labour, I was born. My hearty cries assured my Mummy and Daddy that I was a healthy baby, and the midwife declared me to be perfectly formed with all fingers and toes intact. Timu was not too sure about this new invasion into his life that demanded a lot of attention and made a lot of windy noises. 'This is your sister', he was told, and something in the tone of his Daddy's voice made him think that the burpy little mite was here to stay.

Four weeks later Ernie had a stroke late at night. Irene,

Doris and May took it in turns to sit with him through the nights, holding his hand in a gesture of comfort to both him and themselves. Four days later he died. And four days after the funeral Doris gave birth to her third, perfect baby boy.

Despite Jim's thought that he may not return to work in India they did indeed set sail on the *Chusan* from Southampton docks with me, and the ton of extra luggage I created, in tow.

I loved being a child in India. I loved the open space around the bungalow, the warm sunshine and the freedom to run around in bare feet, all things that I still enjoy to this day. I loved watching the tic-tickys run up the walls or scurry across the veranda, chasing caw-caws with their pointed beaks and shiny black feathers with my big brother. We had to hold our pieces of hot, freshly-baked paratha with both hands to protect it from the birds' preying eyes; they'd swoop down and carry it away if we relaxed our guard. How I miss those parathas. Every morning I would run from our house to my adopted aunties' next-door calling, 'Prata, prate'. My Indian aunt would always greet me with a warm smile and a cuddle, then put a flat circle of the dough she had kneaded onto a hot griddle. Once it was cool enough she'd break it into small pieces and hand them to me. The aunties were three sisters who lived with their father and one brother. They were beautiful young ladies with long, glossy black hair that smelled of coconuts. They showered Timu and me with love and affection, dressed us up in silly costumes and played games with us; we loved them deeply.

Jim often took us to the leper colony in Titagarh. We loved going there where we had many friends. The lady in the white sari, called Mother, held Timu's and my hand as she walked around with us; they were not soft hands like

Irene's but they were large and warm. My most precious memories are of time spent with a man called Praem Chand. He had no fingers or toes and not much of a nose but his eyes were mesmerizing, they were like bright blue jewels that looked deep into mine. Whenever I ran to him he picked me up in his arms and held me tight as I sat on his knee; his smile lit up his whole face. It was he that gave me my new name: he called me Shona Parki, and told me that I was his little bird of paradise. The name caught on and everybody began to call me Shona, everybody but Timu that is, who continued to call me pest.

From stories I'm told, it appears that I was a bit of pest and excelled at causing a disturbance. One day, when I was two years old, we were in Calcutta on the Chowringhee road, a very busy shopping area. I escaped my mother's clutch and took off down an alleyway out of sight, creating havoc with my parents' blood pressures. Jim, oblivious to the injury he could incur upon himself, and in blind panic, threw himself onto his stomach and scoured through the multitude of legs and feet as people stepped over his body. He often recalled and relived the nightmare of trying to find me. It was like searching for a needle in a haystack in a city that resembled the activities of an ants' nest. They yelled my name at the top of their voices but seemingly I tottered along quite unconcerned. Finally Jim caught sight of my chubby little white legs some way in the distance from where he lay on the muddy street. He leapt to his feet and ran, pushing through the crowds of people and rickshaws until he reached me and scooped me up into the safety of his arms.

I loved going to church and singing songs in Hindi. Men sat on the floor with little drums in their hands and they'd pat the drums, making a lovely sound in rhythm with the organ that a man squeezed in and out with one hand and played the keys with his other. Jim would stand at the front of the church and talk, dressed in a long white dress with a black leather belt around his waist and a big wooden cross hanging from a cord around his neck. Sometimes Irene took me to church and she would stand at the front and talk to lots of ladies. Once, as she was talking, I had to sit on a chair on my own and her handbag was left on her chair. I was in front of all the ladies but behind Irene. I began to rummage in her bag and found a toilet roll that I amused myself with as I unravelled it and draped it around my head, face, arms and legs. I tore little holes in the thin paper so that I could see out. People began to giggle and Irene didn't know why. She was not very pleased with me when she turned around to find a little white 'mummy' sitting with the entire contents of her handbag in her lap.

Timu and I had amoebic dysentery most of the time and we couldn't go anywhere without a toilet roll or two. My liver enlarged but Timu's didn't; even so we both had awful medicine to take every day. Irene often gave us injections of vitamin B. We always knew what was coming when Jim put one of us on his knee and cuddled us tightly and began to point to something in the garden. He'd start to talk enthusiastically about the tomato plants, maybe, or the mango tree, and get us to count how many fruits we could see. By the time we'd counted to four the needle was in the upper, outer quadrant of our bottoms, and stinging like crazy. Irene would then rub our skin to disperse the injected fluid and give us lots of kisses.

It wasn't always hot and sunny: sometimes during the monsoon the rain was so heavy that Jim and Timu took a bar of soap onto the back veranda and had a shower in the rain. Ram Smudge used to come out of the cookhouse at the side of the bungalow and stand, fully clothed, in the garden to cool down. He'd turn his face to the sky and let the water wash over him; he didn't much bother with soap though.

None of us were ever very well. We were always getting sore throats, ear aches and running high temperatures with 'flu or tummy upsets. Irene had asthma and a lot of trouble with her sinuses. She went into hospital to have her sinuses washed out. Jim told us that she would be put to sleep and have thin tubes put into her face around her eyes and the doctor would squirt fluid at high pressure through her sinuses. He said she would be very sleepy for a while afterwards but that we could hold her hand gently for a moment then leave her to get over the anaesthetic. But when we were allowed to see her she looked very strange indeed. They hadn't put her to sleep after all and she was nearly crazy with the pain. She didn't smile much at all for a very long time after that.

We went for a holiday; people said that it would do our health good to get some mountain air. Jim set off first with the luggage, two big trunks full. He took a boat across the river from Barrackpore to Serempore station and then a train to Calcutta. Irene took Timu and me in a taxi. We had Blume, our dog, with us too and she was sick on the journey; the taxi driver was not pleased, but Jim placated him when we met at Howrah station. We caught the Madras mail train and settled into the sleeping compartment that we shared with two other men. It was a terrible journey, hot and dusty all the time. I couldn't sleep on the train at all, I kept wriggling and crying. Blume was sick a few times and by the second night Jim and Irene were tired and miserable. They were a bit cross with me for not sleeping but I couldn't help it, I wanted to be outside in the open air. They said that Timu had been a very good boy; I stuck my tongue out at him.

We arrived in Madras at seven o'clock in the morning.

We had the whole day to spend there as our next train was not until eight o'clock that night. We left our luggage in a locked room at the station and went for a spell of sightseeing. We'd never been there before and didn't know our way around. The sun was scorching hot and the city was very busy and crowded. Jim said, 'What are we going to do here with two kids and a dog?' We piled into two rickshaws and went to the beach, but we must have looked a bit strange because soon a crowd of people gathered around us. They just stood and watched us all the time; I don't think they'd seen people with white skin before. In the end we went to a hotel and paid to have a shower and a meal. Jim said it cost a fortune.

We finally arrived, after another overnight train ride, at a place called Mettupalaiyan. We squeezed ourselves into a tiny, crammed, hill train and it took four and a half hours to take us seven thousand feet high into the mountain. When we got there the heavens opened and we got soaked to the skin with rain. But still we had not reached the holiday cottage. We got into a taxi and Jim piled the luggage into a horse-drawn cart and we continued our mountain climb. We were so high up towards the clouds that Jim said, 'Bless me soul, we'll be passing Hillary and Tenzing on their seventh camp'.

The taxi stopped outside a ramshackle hut. 'This is surely not Paradise Cottage', said Irene. But it surely was. It was awful. There were two rooms: one bedroom and a living room with a table and chairs and an empty fireplace. The kitchen was outside in the open air, as was a cold water tap. The toilet was a thunder box. We were soaking wet, freezing cold, very tired and extremely hungry. The luggage bag with all our food in had fallen over on the cart and spilled out, leaving a trail up the mountain. Inside, the cottage was as cold as a fridge. Jim chopped some wood and made a fire in the fireplace and set up a *chulah*, paraffin cooker, to boil water for drinking. We ate a few sweets that were left in the bottom of the bag and went to bed where we froze. We were not happy.

The next morning we all woke up with colds and I excelled myself with one of the worst bouts of dysentery I'd ever had. Jim took Timu on a trek down the mountain in search of provisions and Irene boiled pans of water and spent the day washing clothes and bedding. Despite the state of my tummy I was still very lively and kept playing in the sheets that were hanging up to dry around the room. Irene tried to encourage me to have a rest but I was far too interested in wrapping myself up in the clean, damp sheets. We did have one good day when we went to the government gardens in the town and hired a rowing boat on the lake. Jim and Timu had an oar each and rowed, then later they had a ride on a real horse. We all laughed a lot that day but decided that we wouldn't be taking another hill holiday for a while.

Health-wise, things got a lot worse over the next couple of years. Jim felt that things were moving in the right direction within the circuit, but he was never free from infections and sore throats. The weight just dropped off him and he had no strength and couldn't eat. Irene had become withdrawn and had a faraway look in her eyes a lot of the time. She often fainted and always looked pale. Timu got a series of nasty boils in his ears and the infections made him listless and poorly. My dysentery reached the chronic stage and the strain was telling on Irene. We were sent to live in a house in Shillong, Assam, just before Easter, where Irene could get some support and medical supervision at the missionary hospital. We flew in an aeroplane, for the first time, from Dum Dum airport. On the evening of Easter Sunday Irene was taken into hospital.

She was in for ten days but when she came out she fainted almost every time she stood up. Jim was working in the area so while he was busy the lady who ran the boarding house and who was also the doctor's wife, looked after Timu and me. I was thirsty all the time and was always asking for drinks of water. I developed a peculiar habit of biting the glasses whenever I had a drink. Even though it hurt when the broken glass cut into my lips and filled my mouth with blood I couldn't stop doing it. It caused great consternation to those around me. In the end the lady of the house bought me a thick plastic cup; it soon had an impression of my teeth on the outside, but withstood the attack.

Irene was not herself at all: she was very quiet and cried a lot. They took her to a military hospital to have a special test called an electrocardiograph. Jim was deeply worried about her. The next day the doctor took Jim into his office and talked to him for a long time. Irene, he told Jim, was having a nervous breakdown. Her body had shut down; she'd lost all confidence in herself and was no longer able to function normally. The doctor strongly advised that they resign from their work in India and prepare to return to Britain as soon as possible. He recommended that they stay in Shillong until Irene was fit to travel and that he operate on Jim to remove his tonsils that had been infected for far too long. The doctor was personally going to write a report and send copies to the Missionary Society and the chairman of the district in Calcutta.

Jim had been praying to God and asked that He reveal His will concerning their future through this doctor. When the doctor had said his piece Jim felt it strange that he could show no emotion. 'I am neither surprised nor disappointed', he said, 'I feel no joy or sadness'. Irene received the information in much the same way, but she was afraid, and felt that she was to blame for this outcome. Jim prayed that she would accept the decision as God's will for the family and rest content.

Irene had some bad days. She was full of tears and felt ill. The strain of living in India, with all the illness that came with it, had got too much for her. The doctor had penetrated her defences and exposed the truth that she had never really been happy here, even though she loved the people and the country in general, but the thought of more years here was too much for her. Now that the load had been lifted she felt guilty and could not find peace. Jim concentrated all his effort into reassuring her and believed that when they faced everything together she would get well again. As yet, he was too concerned for his lovely Irene to give a thought to what it meant to him to give up his work.

Jim tried to whip up a little enthusiasm about seeing England again, but the thrill just would not come. He wrote letters to their mothers and hoped they got more of a thrill out of the idea than he did.

Thoughts and questions leapt into his mind: 'Circuit in England, where will I be put? I have no idea what I really want except to serve God. I wonder if there will be any chance of working amongst Indians in Britain. It would be a pity if they could not worship in their own language'. Jim looked through the list of ministerial changes and engagements in a copy of the *Methodist Recorder*. 'Men seem to be changing Church and circuits all the time, I wonder why they move so often. Like rolling stones that gather no moss, how does one grow roots or witness growth?' He lay in the hospital bed, his stomach and bowels empty after the nurse had given him an enema in preparation for his tonsillectomy that was due to happen any moment now. 'What have I achieved in the eight years I have been working in the Mills Area Mission? Nothing! I am only just becoming known in the non-Christian community. I seem to be involved in more problems than I care to think about. I even have my enemies. It is a bad time to have to give up'. He was feeling low but then he lifted his spirits and thought, 'but such giving up is not necessary in England'. Then he read a report on how many ministers had broken under the strain even in Britain. 'Tis a problem, Lord guide the Methodist Church'.

Two nurses appeared and wheeled him into the theatre to await the surgeon. He expected to have an injection that would put him to sleep and grant him glorious oblivion; instead he was given open ether.

When he eventually came round he felt groggy and sick, his head pounded and his throat was filled with pain. Somewhere in the distance he heard the doctor tell him that he hadn't needed any cutting instruments to remove the tonsils. 'They were so badly infected that I just scooped them out with a spoon, they were so full of puss they looked like toothpaste'. 'Lovely', replied Jim hoarsely, 'that's nice'.

Jim was in hospital for twelve days. The infection had been wretched and his body was so weak that the doctor wanted to be sure he was strong enough to hold off further infection before releasing him. When he came back to the house I flung my arms around his leg and cried my heart out. I'd missed my Daddy so much that I didn't know what to do with myself when I saw him. Timu acted far more sensibly: he gave him a big welcoming smile and a hug, but he was older than me of course.

We flew back home to Barrackpore at last and I was very

happy to be home. The aunties had missed us all and baked some fresh parathas in honour of our return. I couldn't wait to go and see Praem the leper and give him a big sloppy kiss on his cheek too. But somehow things were not quite the same. Jim kept going to lots of meetings in Calcutta, he seemed more serious than usual. Irene kept sorting things out all the time and putting everything in piles and writing lists. I didn't much like it at all; surely we were not going on another holiday or to another house.

But apparently we were. In July we went back to Dum Dum airport and got on another aeroplane. At first Jim and Irene had said we were going on a very big ship but the chairman of the district said that none of us were well enough to sail for two weeks, so we must fly.

It was late at night when we flew, and just when we'd got settled and were sleeping, the plane landed and everyone had to get off and walk a long way, through another airport. Jim carried me and Rosebud my dolly, but poor Timu was very tired and he kept sitting on the floor and going back to sleep. We got on another plane and managed to have a nice long, undisturbed sleep. In the morning we arrived at a very busy London airport. Nothing looked familiar to me and nearly everybody had the same white skin as we did and their hair was many different shades and colours, not all black and shiny like at home. There was great excitement when two ladies came running up to us and threw their arms around Jim and Irene, they had lovely smiles and seemed very nice. Two men came and did the same. Timu screwed up his eyes when the ladies kept kissing him. One of the ladies picked me up and kissed and cuddled me as though she knew who I was. There were some boys too, four of them, but they were more interested in watching the planes than us, although they did seem to be fascinated by

Irene's and my saris and Jim's and Timu's long tunics that they wore over their trousers. Really, I didn't know what on earth was going on or who these people were until Jim introduced them to me. 'This is your Auntie Margaret, Auntie Betty, Uncle George and Uncle Joe and these are your cousins, Glynn, Jimmy, Peter and Keith. Ah, now I was getting the picture, these were the people that wrote letters to us and sent parcels of newspapers, and presents of books, and, I pointed to Auntie Margaret, then back to Rosebud, you sent me my dolly.

We all stayed with Betty and George (it was quite a big house) for a week or so and then went by train with Margaret, Joe and Keith to a place called West Hartlepool. There we were met by two older ladies who cried when they saw us. Jim and Irene began to cry too so I thought I may as well join in. Jim pointed to the lady with very white hair and said to me, 'Shona, this is your Gran Parkinson', and then to the lady with grey hair, 'and this is your Grandma Robinson'. A man called Uncle Edwin drove us in his car to Blackhall; it was the biggest and poshest car I had ever seen.

We went to live at Gran Parkinson's house which wasn't far from Grandma's house. Jim and Irene were both very, very ill and Timu and I spent a lot of time at Auntie Margaret and Uncle Joe's house with Keith. We went to the beach a lot and ate lots of fish and chips. Blackhall was very nice and so were my new aunties, uncles, and grandparents. But I couldn't help wondering when we were going home.

DAUGHTER OF A PREACHER MAN

The transitional period in England was confusing. Timu went to school in Blackhall for a short time until Jim was given a temporary position of ministry at Eccleshill in Yorkshire. In India Timu had been the only white boy in school, and here he was still viewed as a foreigner. His skin was still naturally dark from the Indian sunshine and we both spoke with accents, well pronounced English with a flavour of spice. Our sentences were interspersed with Hindi words. Much to our chagrin other children found us to be objects of amusement. In time for the beginning of the new Methodist ministerial year we moved to a small town just outside Bradford in Yorkshire.

While we were still in Blackhall the longing for 'home' lessened because we were surrounded by our new, biological, family. We arrived in Allerton with our little Austin Mini, courtesy of Uncle Edwin, packed full to the brim of belongings. We had no need of furniture as the huge, rambling Victorian house was already equipped with heavy, old-fashioned pieces. I was five and Irene took me to school and told me I'd have a lovely time. I didn't. None of the children were familiar to me and yet they all seemed to know each other very well. I was really not good at sitting still for a long time, it's not the Indian way, but the teacher said that I had to. We were asked to draw a picture of our house, so I drew the bungalow with Ram Smudge and Bloom standing outside looking towards the river at the bottom of the garden. Then we had to draw some people; mine all had brown faces and black hair and the other children laughed at me and said that I was stupid.

The church was a very friendly place with lots of children my own age. Some of them went to my school and I began to make friends. I looked forward to going to Sunday school but I was always a bit miffed when other children were asked to read something out loud during the church service, or play a special part in a play. Once a year there was a special occasion held in the Alhambra Hall in Bradford, and each year a few of the girls were chosen to dress up in beautiful dresses like princesses to represent their Sunday school. The hall was full of girls dressed in long velvet capes, wearing crowns on their heads, escorted by their assistants. I never got to be either Queen or an assistant, apart from one year when one of the assistants was poorly and I had to step in at the last minute. Unfortunately the special dress was too big for me and I had to wear my ordinary Sunday best dress. I looked very out of place.

Irene was still not fully recovered from her nervous breakdown; she was often depressed and had to lie down in bed. Jim was looking a lot healthier and had put on some weight at last. He enjoyed his work at the church and often went to Bradford where many Indian people lived, having moved there from India and Pakistan. Being able to speak their language he was able to help them with their adjustment into the English culture.

Allerton was a lovely place and I loved the view from one of the five attic rooms we had at the top of the house.

From there I could see out across the moors. As well as my friends from the church I had two close friends who lived on our street two doors away from us. They were sisters and they had an older brother who became Timu's best friend. The back of our house had a small garden with a midden, and a gate that opened onto a cobbled back street. After school I played in the street with my friends or we sat on the roof of the midden drawing pictures and dressing our dolls. The boys all played football or cricket and generally ran around chasing each other. At the end of the street a high, dry-stone wall enclosed an orchard that belonged to a farmer. I was a bit of a tom-boy and I loved to climb the wall with the boys, when they let me. We'd play in the long grass of the orchard or swing from a Tarzan-style rope tied to a big sycamore tree. If the farmer caught us in his field he'd shout and chase us with a rifle up against his shoulder and pointed in our direction. During the summer holidays we took off across the fields, only coming home when we were tired and hungry. We girls all wore daisy chain necklaces, that we'd made from picked daisies and threaded together to make a chain around our necks, and buttercups in our hair. Every summer I spent a week or two at Blackhall with my Auntie Margaret.

I loved to go to Hawarth Moor and trample around in the wild heather. Often one of the families from church took me for the day, as Irene was still not well enough to go. I loved to go for walks with Jim. I felt safe and warm when I was with him. We talked a lot on our walks, though often he'd embarrass me terribly by bursting into song in his rich bass voice. He had a lovely voice but I did wish he wouldn't use it when we were out and might be seen by someone from school. 'Dad', I'd implore, 'Dad please stop'. But he'd say that he just couldn't help himself, it was the way he expressed his joy at the beauty of the earth. People that we passed on our walks always acknowledged him respectfully when he had his dog collar on: men raised their hats and ladies smiled and some put on a posh voice when they said hello to him. I didn't like it if someone kept him talking for too long; this was my time with him and I didn't want to share it.

I asked him lots of questions when we walked together, like, 'Why has Timu gone away to boarding school, Dad?'

'Well pet, he's eleven years old now and he's already been to three different schools. At boarding school he'll be able to get an uninterrupted education and be with the same friends all the way through'.

'But why can't he do that here?' I asked.

'Well, because in my job I can't stay in one place for too long, we have to move to new places'.

'Oh. Why does everybody think that we're very rich because we live in such a big house, but I can never have the same things that my friends get because we can't afford them?'

'The house doesn't belong to us, it's just ours to live in while we're here; it comes with the job and my job is more of a vocation than a job to earn a living, clergymen don't get paid a lot of money'.

'Hmmm. Why am I not pretty Dad?' Jim came to an abrupt halt, and bent down to me,

'What makes you think you're not pretty pet, you're very pretty and your pony-tail suits you well'.

'Well why do I never get picked to do things then like read or wear the pretty dresses?' Jim was quiet for a moment before, gently, explaining to me that sometimes, he felt, people deliberately didn't dare choose me in case other people thought they were showing favouritism towards the minister.

'Well why does Mummy not do things with me like other Mummies do with their little girls?' I asked, and wished that I hadn't. Jim looked very sad when he explained that Mummy was very poorly but that one day she'd be better.

*

Religion has played a dominant role in my life, everything revolved around the Church. It dictated where I lived and for how long, it paid no heed to the fact that I was settled in a place and had made friends. When it came time to move to another area of Yorkshire I thought maybe it would be wise for me to go to boarding school as had my big brother. Big mistake. I'd read all Enid Blyton's books on girls' boarding schools and thought they sounded like fun. I was painfully shy and introverted and had not altogether grown out of the habit of biting into glasses. I was also very small for my age and looked quite ridiculous in the uniform that swamped me until Irene, improving in health and disposition, altered it. I'd never learnt to like school anyway, so how I thought I was going to get on when I had to live there as well I don't know.

I didn't get on well at all, there was nowhere to escape to and be alone. Even in bed at night I didn't have a room to myself but shared a dormitory with seven other girls. I missed Jim and Irene dreadfully and felt desperately homesick. The new turquoise, sling-back sandals that Irene bought me, to help make me feel a bit more grown-up, were not allowed and were taken away from me. I hated having to wear two pairs of knickers, thin white ones that we changed every day, worn underneath thick navy-blue ones that we changed twice a week. The thick blue ones came up to my armpits, and as we were all responsible for washing them out ourselves, my white ones turned pale blue.

I lasted less than three years before I packed my marmite sandwiches and ran away one evening with a friend (also a minister's daughter, incidentally). We planned to walk from our school in Scarborough, to Harrogate where Timu was. Very late into the night we grew very scared and had no bearing on where we were. It was dark and raining, and each time a car's headlights caught us in their glare we ducked down at the side of the road to hide, but secretly, we later admitted to one another, we'd hoped that we would be found out. We decided to give ourselves up and knocked on the door of a house and explained what we'd done. The elderly couple were very kind to us, as were the policemen who came to collect us. Back at school the headmistress was not so gentle and understanding. We were made an example of and given a dressing down in front of the whole school. I didn't enjoy it at all.

I was allowed to leave boarding school and move back home with Jim and Irene, except that the market town of Skipton didn't feel like home, I didn't know anybody there. I sat an exam at the local girls' high school, had a guided tour and was introduced to my new teacher. I was due to start after the Easter break. It was many years before I discovered the reason why there had been a sudden change of plan. I did not go to the high school after all but to the local comprehensive. I was no great scholar, by any standards, but my confidence plummeted so low that I became quite withdrawn. I believed that I'd failed the exam and wasn't good enough for the high school, academically or socially. The real reason behind the sudden about turn was that a gentleman and member of the church's congregation, who happened to be on the board of governors at the high school, disagreed with some of Jim's methods and had the power to vent his wrath, indirectly, towards him. There's no sharper way to hurt another human being than to attack a member of their family.

As it happened he did me a favour because I made some very good friends at the comprehensive and was lucky enough to be taught English by a man who inspired me and gave me some much needed confidence.

But why would a person who goes to church and practises Christianity do such a thing as that? Jim and Irene tried to smudge over the whole situation. They came up with reasons why I would be better off and happier going to the comprehensive, which was set in a lovely park and close to the swimming pool, and I did love swimming, I could go after school and I wouldn't have to wear a uniform, although looking back that must have been a worry for them, as they didn't have the money to keep me dressed in the latest fashions. There would be boys to mix with as well as girls. I was happy there but after only one year Jim was told that he was needed to work at a church in London.

Irene was, by now, fully recovered from her nervous breakdown. Jim had nurtured and cared for her with loving, patient compassion. He'd talked with her and prayed for her endlessly. Leaving Allerton, where she'd made lasting friendships, had been a wrench for her, but it was all part and parcel of their joint calling. At Skipton she signed onto a college course and completed a City and Guilds course in dressmaking, tailoring and design. She was very talented and creative and passed with flying colours, making me some very lovely clothes in the process; her confidence lifted and she began to see joy in things around her. She filled the house with flowers and colour.

She and Jim ran a thriving youth group that they were concerned about abandoning. Some of the sixteen-year-olds had begun to leave the church; they were drifting away because they were bored and uninterested. The group met at our house every Sunday evening after the service. It began with five members and grew to over thirty as they invited their friends to come along too. Inspired by the Christian endeavour group they attended in their own youth, Jim and Irene cultivated a friendly and vibrant arena for discussion. The young crowd loved them and confided in them. I loved it, at first, when they all piled into the kitchen noisily, but then when they all went into the huge lounge to start the evening I felt shut out because I was not old enough to join in. I was fiercely jealous of the relationship they shared with my parents, and of all the laughter that went on behind a door that was closed to me. I was beginning to think that I didn't much like this whole church thing anymore. The only other girls of my age that went to church were from the high school and I went to the lowly, comprehensive. None of my school friends had ever been to church other than for weddings or christenings.

I caused a huge fuss when told that we were moving again. I was fourteen and had a happy social life that I didn't want to leave. Jim was deeply distressed for me but knew that he had no choice. He and I took a train to London and went to visit Southall. I saw a spark come into his eyes as we got off the number 207 bus in the centre of a town filled with dark-skinned people with glossy black hair. We walked along South Road and he marvelled at the shops displaying saris and brightly coloured jewellery. We passed a cinema advertising Indian films and heard Indian music drifting from passing cars. He greeted people he passed in Hindi and had an air of excitement about him that I hadn't noticed for a long time. Memories of living in India were, by this time, in my distant past, but something triggered within me. I got a thrill from the vibrant, random, spontaneous lack of order on the streets and I felt a strange sense of belonging. Jim rubbed his hands together and his face burst into a big grin. He turned to me and winked. Suddenly I knew that I was going to like it here.

School, however, was a disaster. My education was in a mess. Somewhere along the line I had completely lost the plot. From the early days in Allerton I'd had more days off sick than ticks for attendance. Only a short time after I'd first started school I had an accident and fell off the top of a monkey bar in a physical education lesson. I landed on my head and knocked myself clean out. I became prone to fainting, particularly when anxious or distressed which, with all the moves and changes, was pretty much all the time. I found going to a new school at fourteen horrible. It's not that my new peers were unfriendly, they were not, but I found it very difficult to pick up the thread of what was being taught. I became very anxious and dreaded going and was passing out all over the place. The mere sight of a school door had me crumbling to the ground. Although an electroencephalogram showed that I had some weird things going on in my brain, not epilepsy and thankfully not wiggly worms, but some reaction to the fall from the monkey bar, an interesting little chat with a psychiatrist led him to believe that I had a few psychological problems and he declared me to be school phobic. I was very happy indeed when I was told that I had been granted exemption from the educational system at the age of just fifteen.

It would be very true to say that being a daughter of the manse has played a role in tipping the fragile balance of my disposition. It would be fair to say that my religious, church dominated upbringing has screwed me up. Jim and Irene were both full-time workers for God and the Church and there have been a great many times that I have resented the intrusion of the Church into our family life. Children of clergymen have to share their parents with many people. They have to accept that Dad does not come home from work at six o'clock in the evening to switch off, relax and offer his undivided attention. Contrary to the beliefs of many, parsons do not have a cushy little job and only work on Sundays. Until recently they didn't even have one day off a week, they are at the beck and call of many, often day or night. I can hardly remember a meal-time that was not disturbed by a telephone call.

Because the boundaries between work and home are so vague, children cannot help but pick up on their parents concerns. The manse was often like living in a goldfish bowl, restricting but visible to close scrutiny. Church committees are run by nominated volunteers. There are some very honourable and noble people of great faith and integrity on such committees; there are also some meddling, picky and power-obsessed folk who revel in being awkward. Such people had no qualms about turning up at the manse, unannounced or uninvited, to voice their criticisms to the minister in his own home. They seemed to neither understand nor care that the children of the house may be able to hear such outbursts and feel deeply, deeply hurt to hear their beloved father spoken to in such unnecessarily rude tones. Jim could handle such situations, I could not and I took them to heart. Many, but not all, children of the clergy that I have spoken to, share similar reactions to mine, having been, on occasion, pushed into second place by the Church. I personally know of quite a few who have turned their backs on all religions and churches in bitterness and resentment, filled with confusion, not just about Church as an organisation but about the guilt that results from such an intensely religious upbringing.

Oddly, or so it seems to me now, I never blamed God for how I felt. I never went to the top with my grievances; after all, God is God. I don't think I equated Him, Her, It with the problem. The Church was my problem, the Church, its problems, its people and its people's problems were what filled the air of any house I lived in. I didn't understand, or rather recognise, as a child, that this calling to live a life of devotion to the Church was really a calling of devotion to God, a life that pulled those who accepted the challenge of the call into a life somewhat apart from the norm. The children born to acceptors of the challenge become, themselves, not of the norm. I didn't associate God or religion with the Church. During my childhood, dog-collared clergymen were highly respected people in the community. Even some of the roughest diamonds at school would never swear in front of me or if they did they would be nudged and told, 'Hey, you can't say that, her Dad's the vicar'. I just wanted to be normal.

Jim was not oblivious to my problems, it troubled him greatly that I did not feel what I perceived to be normal. He had an awful lot on his plate when we were children. On top of his work he had to be husband and carer to Irene during her struggle with depression, mother and father. It cannot have been easy for him and my never ending pleas for not wanting to go to school each day must have been a trial.

My happy childhood memories are of great camping holidays, flying kites, playing French cricket, swimming and identifying wild flowers, along with wonderful, fun filled times when the family got together. Times with Gran and Grandma, the aunties, uncles and cousins were very precious. At such reunions Irene smiled a lot and Jim's laughter filled the air. But the most treasured memory I have was on a warm, sunny Sunday afternoon. On an impulse, in the morning before going to church, Jim decided that we wouldn't put the roast in the oven but that we would come home and pack a picnic. 'We'll make some sandwiches and go to Manningham Park', he announced. 'You can miss Sunday school today'. My heart soared. I sat in church and willed the service to be over quickly; my excitement threatened to overwhelm me.

We drove into Bradford and carried the picnic bag, a rug and a ball into the park. We found a nice spot to lay down the rug and I bit into my tomato sandwich; the bread was soggy and delicious with juice. After we'd eaten, Jim and Timu, who was home on holiday from boarding school, and I played football; even Irene joined in. The park was full of picnicking families, many of them Indian, the ladies in saris and the men in long white cotton shirts. We walked around the park and admired the flowers; Irene knew the names of them all. My heart was full to bursting with joy. It was all so outrageously, blissfully, rapturously normal.

JOY

I may sound embittered about my role as the daughter of the manse, I'm not, I'm just trying to paint the picture of how it was through my eyes while trying to decipher how I reached the point where I'm at now. It may appear that I resent my parents for the way and the environment in which they brought me up; I most certainly do not. I wouldn't have swapped them for anything, or anyone in the world; they were honourable, caring and deeply loving people and parents. If it appears that I have been confused by my role and identity, then yes, I have.

My husband is a chartered accountant but I don't introduce myself as an accountant's wife because his profession has not shaped me into who I am. Thankfully people don't expect me to know the workings of balance sheets, audits and tax returns, so why then did people I met as a teenager assume that I could quote chapter and verse of the Bible? I could not then and I still cannot now. Indeed, when I first met Rock he thought my Dad was a member of parliament, so immersed was I in the life of the manse that it never occurred to me that he may not even know what a minister was. Once his mates learned that I was the equivalent to a vicar's daughter the jokes rolled, but believe me I'd heard them all before.

What perplexes me is why we children of clergy were expected to 'know better'. If, as a group of children we were playing and maybe being a bit naughty, why did I have to be singled out and pointed the finger at because, 'and you, you really should know better'. Excuse me, why was I expected to know better, and know what better anyway? Such high and unrealistic expectations thrust guilt upon childish shoulders. Another perplexity that carried a weight of guilt is the 'nice' little rhyme that was often taught, parrot-fashion, along the way, joy: 'J' for Jesus, 'O' for others and 'Y' for yourself, Jesus comes first, then others and lastly, you, or in this case me. The message of JOY alongside the command to be humble and not worthy is, in my 'humble' opinion, too complex for children to grasp. On the one hand we're taught to love others as we love ourselves and then we're given the message to put ourselves right at the back of the queue. What a conundrum.

As I got older I held, not consciously or willingly, onto the image of myself as a minister's daughter. Such was the effect of our family role that I couldn't leave it behind and grow into *me*. Childhood Sundays were busy days. First we'd all go to morning service, although obviously we couldn't sit together because Dad was preaching either at our church or somewhere in the district; then in the afternoon Timu and I walked along to Sunday school. But many is the time, as I watched my friends go home to have tea with their families and maybe play a board game together, that we all went to somebody else's house for tea where, without a shadow of a doubt, and I really don't mean to offend anybody's feelings here, a great big bowl of cold banana custard would have been prepared for my benefit. I really, really do not like banana custard, and as being polite was integral to my role I never found the courage to say 'no thank you'. Poor Mum would try her best to rescue me but I dutifully took it upon myself to accept a portion and gag my way through it. She did, however, put her foot down if I was offered a drink in a glass, unless I was taken alone into our host's kitchen behind her back. In those instances, upon hearing the scream she would realise that I had bitten out a chunk and was now pouring with blood.

It's as though I have been trapped in a time warp. I am an adult and I act in an adult way, well most of the time anyway, I'm a mother and a lover, I've held down responsible jobs and yet a part of me held onto the little girl in the huge Victorian manse. I never enjoyed going to church really and I could come up with multiple excuses to avoid it. In a discussion with Jim, when I was in my early thirties, he mentioned his observation to me by pointing out that he'd noticed that I didn't include church on Sundays as part of my regular routine. He noted that I went when it suited me rather than by recognising that on a Sunday morning I get ready and go to church. He was correct. He wasn't criticising me or telling me off, simply observing. But I fully suppose that it made him sad. Not sad because I wasn't doing what he wanted me to do, but sad because his life of loving and serving God had brought him a wealth of fulfilment. He urged me to question my beliefs and come to my own conclusions but at that point in time I could raise no questions; God was God, I loved Him, and church was where one goes to worship, but maybe not every week. All I can offer in my defence is that I wanted to believe and was happy to believe, but I accepted his beliefs as my own and yet, if I'm brutally honest with myself, I now realise that I didn't even bother to really question his theology in its nitty-gritty form.

While on a family holiday in Florida, with Rock and our

two children, I followed a ridiculous urge to have a go on a waterslide called, the 'Bomb bay drop'. I followed a young, fearless boy up the steps and watched as he entered the door of the little hut at the top. I couldn't see into it but was a little alarmed at the speed with which he came out of its bottom. A strapping, deeply tanned and muscular life-guard smiled at me as he opened the door to allow me in for my turn. With horror I noticed that there was no seat to sit on and prepare myself for descent. The life-guard registered my querying look and explained to me that I was to stand in the little square and place my arms across my chest, Egyptian mummy style but without an 'ankh' to safe guard my journey.

'Why must I do this', I asked.

'So that you don't catch your arms on the sides and injure yourself Mam', he explained in a matter of fact tone. I realised, too late, that actually I didn't really want to go down this slide but as I looked out of the small window to protest the young man smiled back and put up his thumb to signify time for off.

'Oh-mi-god!' I yelled from the bottom of my lungs as the floor beneath my feet dropped open and plunged me, like a woman at the gallows, down seventy-two feet of blue plastic. The act had my adrenalin pumping wildly, filling me with an intoxicating fusion of thrill and fear. Coming a close second to that experience, though on a mental level, was when I began to search, putting any presuppositions of God behind me. What is God to me, indeed if there is a God at all? In place of what is God to my father and therefore indirectly to me?

A number of events put me onto this search, when my teenage children wanted to know if I thought I would still be religious if Gran and Grandpa had not been. I didn't have an answer for them or myself. When I was reminded of Sigmund Freud's observation in his book, Totem and Taboo, *'Psychoanalysis of individual human beings teaches us with quite special insistence that the God of each of them is formed in the likeness of his Father, that his personal relationship to God depends on the relation to his Father in the flesh, and oscillates and changes along with that relation, and that at bottom God is nothing other than an exalted Father',* I felt very disturbed indeed. I adore my father, he is my hero. Is he then the God of my making? Someone who is always there for me, who loves me unconditionally no matter what I do?

The horrible death of my lovely Mum really floored me and sowed the first seed of doubt. Don't misunderstand me, I did not blame God for her death, I was too busy railing at the ineptitude of the hospital concerned. It was the lack of peace that emanated from her that brought the first niggle of uncertainty. I couldn't make myself go to church after that because the disturbing question of her peace was rocking my equilibrium and keeping me awake at night, but I never told anybody what she had said or how I felt. It ate away, painfully, inside me.

Events happen of course. Extremists start to throw bombs around, innocent people get killed or maimed, and it's all claimed to be in the name of God, for God. My own daughter stepped onto the tube at King's Cross station in London in 2005, she turned around to make sure her flatmate had followed her and huffed impatiently when she found that she had not. She stepped back off the tube onto the platform and a few moments after the doors closed in front of her the bomb, in the very carriage she had entered, exploded. I thanked God profusely for saving her life, but what of all the others who were not saved? It's true that at that point it was my parents that had saved their granddaughter. The vision was dramatically clear in my mind: Jim and Irene, in translucent form, took hold of her and pulled her back from the tube into safety. Yes, I was convinced, what a comforting scene.

Things didn't get much easier that year. Rock and I went on holiday to Corfu in search of respite. Our son was on holiday in Spain with some friends and our daughter had come home for a break from her job experience in London as part of her university course. At the end of the first week we were awakened, at four-thirty in the morning local time, by the ringing of Rock's mobile phone. Our little girl was crying heartily and trying, through her sobs, to tell us that we had been burgled. I had a new car, a flash one; the kids had convinced me that it was time I had a bit of fun, leave my overriding sense of practicality and go for something with a bit of panache. This car fit the bill. Unfortunately other people thought so too and instead of admiring it they decided they would take it. Two cars blocked it in on our driveway, our son's and one of our daughter's friends. The thieves smashed the windows of both cars that were in the way and released the hand brakes to push them onto the garden. They broke into the house, via the dining-room window, and set about taking everything that took their fancy, including our daughter's laptop with all her university work stored in it and my laptop with the first draft of this very book. Our daughter had back up, thankfully; so did I, but for some reason they decided to take that as well, it's probably lying in a ditch somewhere all soggy and wet. They did find the keys to the car and drove it away, but I think the most heartless thing they did was to take all the prettily wrapped presents that were intended for our daughter's birthday which was on the very next day. I am so thankful that she was out that night for an early celebration. The horror she found on her return home was extremely unpleasant. So if you're out there thieves, I have gone back to a practical car and the keys are under the mat.

Is it greed that causes people to steal what belongs to another? Greed possibly born out of need, or maybe dependence on drugs that many feel they need in order to cope with life in this often confusing world we live in. I'm not sure where the blame lies for the state of hospital wards, be it government cut-backs on spending, lack of disinfectant or, more worryingly lack of genuine care? I have no idea what causes a human being to put a bomb in their rucksack and kill many innocent people along with themselves, other than perhaps a fanatical and distorted grasp of honouring God and religion. But as I have discovered, it is so easy to get bogged down in troubling dimensions of religions and the effects they have on our lives that I find it no wonder so many people get confused and so many reject any concept of a God. How must it look to a homeless heroin addict, an abused, neglected child or a person demented by loneliness and fear as I stand, finely dressed in church and sing hymns of adoration and love on a Sunday, then go home to my roast dinner and smile, feeling good that I've attended that week and done my obedient duty to God. I've prayed for those who suffer and I've prayed for peace in the world, my sins have been confessed and forgiven so I can now look forward, fearing not death because I have been given the promise of eternal life to look towards, and the delight of being reunited with my loved ones who have passed before me. I do care as I sing and pray, I really care and feel sorrow for the plight of many, but what am I doing about it? Do my prayers and my church attendance help them?

If I am to claim a belief in and a love for God then I am not free to sit back on my laurels in apathy, I am bound to a responsibility to explore and discover the message that God gives and to act upon that message. And if Jesus is the only way that I can get to God then I'm thrown into a whole other whirlwind of confusion because that way the people of other religions are excluded, and I do not know if I can accept that.

THE PAIN OF LOSS

After my mother's death, during the period when I felt that the world should have stopped turning, I bumped into an acquaintance of hers. On hearing the news she stood tall and threw her arms wide exclaiming, 'Oh how wonderful. Don't be sad because she's happy now, she's with your Dad and they are together again'. Her face was wreathed in smiles and her expression was one of genuine joy.

I don't feel that I can put down in black and white the words that came into my mind, for at that moment I felt swamped with outrage. Shock rocked the very core of my being. I felt the lady's comment to be totally inappropriate; how dare she disregard my Mother's loss of life and my own personal suffering at the tragedy of death. I said nothing in return but stumbled home clutching my arms to my chest.

My children called my mother Grannybugs, because for them the name fitted their image of her which was a loving lady full of laughter, fun and mischief. It was she who built snowmen with them and took them to pick the shiniest conkers. She who played endless games such as how many words can you think of beginning with such and such a letter of the alphabet, to make learning and spelling a jolly affair. It was she who taught them how to bake walnut biscuits and then had them fighting over who was going to do the washing-up, because she turned that task into fun too. Irene Mary Parkinson's initials spelt IMP, and she was, in her later years, just that, a cute little 'imp' with a twinkle in her eyes.

I was afraid, after her beloved Jim died, that the light within her would turn out. But no, she continued to live and function to the best of her ability. Obviously she had moments when she temporarily broke down, on hearing a certain song for example. One day as she sat in my car Louis Armstrong's voice came over the radio waves singing, *'We have all the time in the world'*, and tears dripped from her eyes because of course, she and her husband no longer had any further time together. Another song that set her off was Barry Manilow's *I can't smile without you*, because as she arrived at Jim's bedside in hospital one morning, he'd beamed his smile towards her and told her that he'd just heard that very song through his headphones and cried when the words, *I'm finding it hard to leave your love behind me*, flowed into his ears. Their tears honoured the love they had shared.

I took Mum out for lunch one day and she lost her footing on a step no higher than two inches. I recall the scene that followed vividly as she fell forward, as though in slow motion, and landed with a thud, hitting the top of head on an opposing wall. I still hear my own voice calling out to her as I ran to her aid, I still see the blood that trickled from the corner of her eye and seeped into the collar of her knitted coat. She'd broken a bone at the top of her spine in that fall and spent two months lying flat on her back in a hospital bed with an ugly and cumbersome brace fastened around her neck. When I was told that she'd broken her neck I was horrified, and imagined her future to be that of a quadriplegic. Remarkably and thankfully that was not the case. Little by little the position of her bed was raised and each day she began to be thrilled by the new line of vision that began to grow in her sight. After weeks of staring at the same ceiling, which offered a distinct lack of stimulation or inspiration, she marvelled at the joy of being able see what was going on around her instead of having to conjure up a picture of happenings in her mind. After spending the summer months in a smaller hospital for longer term treatment she was able to go back to her own home.

When Jim and Irene retired from their work in Southall, after sixteen years there, they moved to my home town in Worcestershire because at that time Timu and his wife had no children and were undecided as to the permanence of their location. After a year or two it happened that we ended up living next-door to one another, for which I was thankful as it became obvious that Irene was going to need help if she were to manage living in her own surroundings, which she very much wanted to do. Her broken neck, we were informed, was not going to heal and no operation could be performed to improve her situation, and the risk involved in an attempt may have resulted in making it worse. So there it was. She had the choice of giving up on life or getting on with it. She chose to get on with it and had to swallow her independent pride and allow us to push her around in a wheelchair whenever we went out. She was able to potter around her house with the aid of a walking frame and a stair-lift transported her, giggling all the way, upstairs. She was coping and I was happy to care for her; the whole family pulled together to help.

What I have trouble in dealing with is the way in which she suffered when she was admitted to hospital for some tests because she had become frail and her legs had weakened to the extent that she began to fall over. Why, I ask, in this twenty-first century has hospital care deteriorated to such a degree that patients have suffered, and in many cases, died? When it was decided that Irene may benefit from a spell of observation in hospital we were delivered to the accident and emergency department for an overview of her condition and needs. I was asked to hand over any medication that we had with us at that time; this I did and this I still deeply regret. We were put in a room and left there for approximately four hours, during which time we were occasionally visited by a series of doctors who repeated the same questions as the one who had come before. At home Irene had been taking prescribed strong pain-killers, to relieve the intensity of pain caused by the effects of the broken bone in her neck. The bone at the top of the spine has a little peg on it to hold the head in place; it was that little peg that had broken off in the accident, leaving her head precariously balanced on top. I'm sure that a member of the medical profession may argue the reality of her head actually falling off but that's how the doctors originally explained the break to me. Consequently she had to wear a collar around her neck at all times.

It took many pillows or cushions to get Irene into a position of comfort and as there were none available in the department we were left in, or so we were told, she was in extreme pain. I asked for pain-killers to be given to her but was told, 'not until the doctor gives permission'. I asked if they could give her one of her own tablets that she had after all been taking for some time with great success, but was told 'no'. I felt utterly helpless and responsible as my Mum lay on that hard examination couch for such a long time in agony. Her body shook, she became disorientated and confused that I was not giving her the tablets that would have brought relief. When at last, six hours after our arrival, a very pleasant and caring young male doctor attended to her and administered pain relief, Mum, within a short time, was laughing again. Timu and I were utterly fraught with tension, worry and concern. Many are the times that I wished I had wheeled her out of the hospital there and then.

Being a nurse herself Irene had no fear of hospitals, in fact I would go so far as to say that she felt quite excited when she had occasion to visit one, as it revived her fond memories of bustling about the wards in her younger days. Within a week of her stay I noticed that the spark had gone out of her eyes; she said all the 'right' things and never complained but I could tell she was troubled. I received a telephone call from the ward at five o'clock one morning and told I had better go straight in to see my Mum as she had had a fall and her heart was failing. 'How could she have fallen in the corridor?' I asked, 'she's not supposed to be out of bed and walking'. I was told that she must have been going to the bathroom, and as the discussion progressed it became apparent that the night staff didn't even know that she had a broken neck. From that day on things went from bad to worse. I arrived at visiting time to find her in a subdued state. I knew something was wrong and I coaxed her into telling me what it was. After the fall in the corridor the night duty staff had wheeled her bed into the corridor by the reception desk so that they could keep an eye on her. Unfortunately the staff were very busy that night, so the only times that Irene saw a nurse was when one whisked by her on their way to do something. She was left alone with no buzzer to call for attention and no water to drink or to wash down the tablets she was given at the allotted time. She did ask for water, but it never arrived; she asked for a bed pan when she needed one, but it never arrived either. She lay all night, for three nights in a row parched, with the bitter taste of tablets that were stuck in her throat, in a wet bed because she could not get to the loo. She suffered needless humiliation and loss of dignity.

Irene had been in hospital for almost four weeks when Christmas morning dawned and by this time I was going to see her first thing in the morning and staying until evening because I was too concerned to leave her alone. Too often her food and drinks had been put on her table but not within her reach, then cleared away before anyone had got around to helping her eat. The same was happening to other patients on the ward but all were afraid to complain in fear of the consequences.

A notice was placed in the entrance to the ward one day informing all visitors that we must put on a plastic apron and wash our hands both on arrival and on departure. Each time we left the ward we were required to throw the apron away and replace it with a new one on return. When I asked the reason for the aprons I was told that it was nothing to worry about, just a little bug that's going around and the apron will help prevent it from travelling outside of the ward. I called into the supermarket on my way home one evening, I'd said goodbye to one of the nurses on duty as she stood by the sink in the ward, rubbing a mark off her uniform with a paper towel. As I made my way from the checkout I noticed the same nurse pick up a basket, wearing her uniform dress with an open jacket on top, and make her way to the fruit and vegetable section. Shortly before I'd left the ward another nurse had spilt some of the liquid contents from a bed-pan onto the floor. When I walked in to see Mum the next day a sticky patch on the floor lay in the same place where the spill had dripped the evening before, and the nurse I'd seen in the supermarket still had the same mark on her uniform that she'd attempted to remove with a paper towel.

The 'little bug' that was not to be worried about was *clostridium difficile*, referred to as C diff by the staff, and it found its way into Irene. Her abdomen was distended and fiercely painful to the touch and she lost control of her bowels. Over the next few weeks I watched my mother age almost beyond recognition as the weight fell from her small frame; the form of her skeleton was visible through her papery thin skin and the tips of my thumb and third finger touched easily around her ankles.

On a cold February morning I walked across the car-park and made my way up to my mother's bedside in a ward on the second floor of the hospital that I am choosing not to name. (The reason that I have decided not to name and shame is that some people have received excellent treatment there and also because I am led to believe that improvements are being put in place and I have no desire to frighten anybody faced with the prospect of admittance). I sat down beside my Mum and took her bony hand in mine; she turned to me and in a gentle tone she said, 'I don't think I'm going to last much longer pet'. I felt the breath catch in my throat and my heartbeat quicken. I knew in that moment it was imperative that I remain calm, even though a scream was threatening to force itself from my windpipe. I brought to mind all the passages of assurance I had heard read and the hymns I'd sung, the words of comfort that had flowed in abundance on the peace of at last meeting with one's maker. I brought to mind the Bible texts that she had carefully written in silver ink against black paper and stuck on the wall of her living-room to support her during periods of struggle or self-pity. I asked Mum gently, but also with an expectant air of certainty at her response, 'Do you feel at peace?' When she answered my question with a weak and wispy, 'no', the room appeared to spin around and I felt myself to be whirling like water rushing down a plughole; but somehow I managed to stay in control and followed the doctor, at his request, into an empty room where he told me that he was going to pass Mum into the hands of the palliative care team.

Because I did not pursue the question of her peace, or rather lack of it, because she, from that moment on drifted into a speechless state, I find myself left in a tormenting and restless place with a head full of questions that nobody else can answer for me. I am filled with regret that I did not urge her to explain her own tormented state of mind. I have always been susceptible to feelings of guilt and have struggled to forgive myself. Jim used to urge me not to post-mortem but instead to learn by my mistakes, actions and events and then let them go. I still find that to be sound advice in many areas of my life but in the case of Mum's peace I'm not sure and I carry a weight of guilt. I have learnt that if I'm faced with a query I will question it no matter how stupid my question may sound; my family will verify that fact. But watching my Mum die in such a way has left me unable to let her go.

I greet the framed photograph in my study on a daily basis and smile back at my father who stands with his hands on his hips and beams his infectious, all-embracing smile and I feel happy and so proud that he was my Dad. It's true that he's no longer here beside me but his spirit lives on in my heart and I'm reminded of all that he has left behind him, his joy, his zest for life, his compassion, integrity and never-ending quest for justice, and most of all his genuine love. By remembering, valuing and honouring the attributes of my Dad Jim, and the way that I am very often told that he touched people's lives and made a difference, I can feel that his time on earth was not in vain and that in a way he still lives on. I realise that by looking at the photograph of Mum, as she lay in a hospital bed with a ghastly collar around her neck, a drip in her arm and an oxygen mask over her nose, that I have simply let her die.

Why, I ask myself, can I not let go? I am still not at the stage when I can put her smiling face and laughing eyes next to Dad to greet me each day. I hold onto the most ridiculous 'things' in her memory. Each day as I went into her house via the back door I passed through what she and Dad called the cabin. It was a half-glazed, half timber building that housed the washing machine, but it also had the effect of a conservatory so on a summer afternoon the two of them would sit in there, with sunshine pouring in, and either rest or read. When it came time to clear out their home after their deaths I fell apart as I picked up the plastic tub of washing tablets that stood on the shelf. Because I could see that tub when I looked through my bedroom window towards the cabin it became, for me, a significant reminder of her being alive, perhaps because whenever I loaded her washing into the machine she reminded me where to put the tab. Now if my family are reading this they may look in the cupboard of our utility room and check the tub that I keep our washing tabs in. Yes, they will find the brand that I buy emptied into the old tub of the brand that Mum used to prefer. If my brother, Timu reads this he will probably shake his head in wonder and, quite rightly, tell me off, as would Mum if she knew.

It's easy to forget the annoyances as I watch a mother and daughter sharing time with one another in a coffee shop. I miss those times when we lingered and chatted, but funny how no more do I remember the exasperation I sometimes felt on a weekly trip to a supermarket that could take up to three hours of meandering up and down the aisles before we even got close to the aroma of coffee. It takes little to bring on the onset of tears when I miss the happy things and yet I feel really bad if the frustrations come into my mind: how Mum would insist that we allow an hour to get to an appointment when fifteen minutes would see us there in time for instance. Dad annoyed me plenty, of course, by always wanting to know where I was going and what I was doing, or by refusing to pay the price in a café for a sandwich and instead making beetroot sandwiches for us both and insisting that we eat them on a bench in the middle of Oxford Street. I can laugh at Dad's offences, but the difference is that although I will never stop missing his physical presence I have allowed him to die and have laid him to rest. Until I can laugh, really laugh, at Mum's annoying little ways, I can see that I am keeping her in a no-longer-alive and yet not-quite-dead state of being, and in so doing I am paying her no honour.

I feel angry that Mum died in the early hours of the morning; having been by her side for most of her waking moments, why did she die when I was not there? I don't know who it is that I feel angry with, Mum herself perhaps for not waiting for me, the hospital for not calling us in time, God, or simply myself for having failed her in her last moments of need and not bidding her a final goodbye? I worry that Mum felt alone and scared at the end and wondered why none of us were there to hold her hand. I can only console myself with the sure knowledge that she did at least know how dearly she was loved as she passed away.

The family tease me that I am getting more and more like my Mum every day. Following the years of her depression she fell in love with colour, influenced by the years spent in

India, and became a little zany in her style of fashion. I can't admit to dressing flamboyantly, yet, but I have become more adventurous with the colour schemes in our home by adding the odd touch of fluorescent fuchsia pinks and bright, zesty limes. I've taken to writing many lists and keeping my finances and filing in meticulous order, just as she did, and as organisation has never been my strong point I'm finding her guidance all rather helpful. I have restrained from enlarging her collection of elephants but I do wish the sight of one would stop making me cry.

A SILENT WHISPER

Despite my childhood and adolescent feelings towards the Church I did continue to attend on a regular basis throughout my teenage years. The church in Southall somehow became very special to me. Whether it was solely the multi-racial aspect I don't know, but like the town itself the church had an open and welcoming air about it. Perhaps it was because I saw that my parents were able to fully engage in their calling and work with their gifts to act on their sympathies. But I was encouraged by the work and loving community of both the Asian-and English-speaking congregations of the church to enter into Christian training. So as a wide-eyed enthusiastic eighteen-year-old I left home to study the Bible and doctrines of the Christian life. During an intense year of study and communal living in a beautiful rambling old building, snuggled amongst the rolling hills of Derbyshire, I made some loving friendships and forgot what the outside world was like. In retrospect I realise that I was neither mature enough nor sufficiently inquisitive towards my personal beliefs to endure it.

The community of students was made up of young people who felt they knew a personal relationship with God. The purpose of the course was to seek a sound knowledge of the Bible and so gain spiritual direction. I thought I had a relationship with God, well, He had certainly been a central character in my life. I used all the right words, I asked God to come into my heart, to forgive my sins and have mercy upon me. I wanted to understand the Bible and its message, I wanted to serve the Lord and encourage others to know His love. For the first six months I had never been happier in my life. But then, about three-quarters of the way through the course I remember realising, as I lay on my narrow bed staring up at the ceiling, that I was no longer thinking. The thought came as a jolt and I didn't like it. The dialogues that naturally took place in my head had ceased to take place. Nothing was going on in there, I wasn't mulling things over, I was simply absorbing all that drifted towards me from the front of the classroom. I realised that I was living on an even plane with no ups and no downs. I had no inner conflicts because I accepted all that I was being taught without question. I soaked up the words and opinions of the lecturers like a sponge and was terrified of getting anything wrong. I took their view on things on board, rather than seeking to explore and examine my own feelings and interpretations. I began to spout the religious language fluently, though clearly without proper understanding. I had it in my head that what I was being taught was correct, leaving no room for compromise. I even started to write letters to my brother who was a student at London University, and I added nice little chapter and verse quotes from the Bible at the end. He never replied. It was, again in retrospect, as though my conscious thinking mind had packed its bag and cleared off.

In an effort to regain control of my thoughts I began to skip mealtimes in the communal dining-room. I stopped going to the coffee shop where I ate scrumptious homemade cakes with my friends. Instead I bought tubs of cottage cheese and took them with a spoon, each day, for a walk by a stream. I enjoyed the brief spells of solitude, but my intention to soul search in peaceful surroundings got swamped by the discovery that my jeans had begun to hang from my bony frame. I'd always been slim but had put on a few pounds by eating the food served in the college dining-room. It took very little time to shed the pounds on my new diet of fruit and cottage cheese, and before I realised what was happening my need for space and solitude had turned into a journey of self starvation and I didn't know how to turn back. I promised myself that I'd stop when the pointer reached five stones on the scales, but of course I didn't. I furiously denied the doctor's diagnosis that I had anorexia nervosa and my outburst confirmed his suspicion. A long and tormenting struggle ensued. I could see looks of horror pass across the faces of my friends and family but I couldn't understand their concerns because I didn't see myself as thin at all.

My parents treated me with tender patience but my emotions were volatile and I argued aggressively that all was well and would be even better if I could just lose another few pounds. My entire life centred on weighing-scales and food. Although I wouldn't eat food, I prepared wholesome meals and baked rich gateaux for anybody who would eat them. Eventually I did begin to eat and everybody thought I was healed until my Mum discovered that I was making myself vomit after every single morsel of food that I ate.

When my condition did improve I came out of the dark tunnel smiling and still claiming to be a Christian who thanked God for healing. On the basis of my college grounding and qualifications I took a job that called for an applicant who was a committed Christian to live and work alongside the British Army in Germany. I can see now that I got that job on the basis of my use of religious language during the interview. I spoke with sincerity but did I really understand what I was confessing in the spirit of Christianity? I think not, because I was totally unprepared for the job. I was never questioned about how I would manage to put my devotion to the Lord into practice in the situation that I was in, literally, flown into by an army aeroplane. I was not equipped to handle myself amongst a couple of thousand men, many of whom were lonely and longed for the comfort of family. I worked long hours in a role that, to this day, I have still not figured out, doing a variety of tasks both clerical and manual. In my role I talked and listened to the problems and tales of many soldiers, but mostly I ended up in a romantic mess, being a young single girl surrounded by soldiers in uniform who charmed me with their attentions.

My Christianity has been integral to my life but as I look back over the years I see my naivety and lack of depth and maturity towards my faith. I have been so immersed in the lifestyle and rituals of Christianity, and so caught up in a net of what's morally right and wrong in scriptural terms that I have been bound in guilt. When I 'sinned' I suffered in deep torment. As a teenager living in London I had many avenues of entertainment within my reach and I enjoyed a healthy social life but the Bible, and the Church, followed me around like a shadow and poked me frequently in the conscience. It's not as though I wish that hadn't been the case, for I respect moral boundaries, but the Sunday-school-taught boundaries remained rigid and heavy. I neither found the conviction to totally rebel against religion nor to submerge myself fully within it, because to a certain degree I remained mindless. I floated along in a bubble of belief, free of challenge. It was a safe yet ineffectual place to be. It is a sad fact of my life that I never truly found myself because I was probably playing the role of what I was, a minister's daughter.

*

As winter began to blossom into early spring and the sympathy cards in honour of my mother had been packed into a box, I took an indulgent lone trip to Cornwall in search of solace. I wasn't afraid of wild tigers on the run during that drive because the route was very familiar to me, having spent many family holidays in the south west of England. Also, because I was so consumed with grief there was little space left in my head to worry about anything. I've always been the type of person who feels a need to be alone for a while. Maybe it began when I wandered down an alleyway in Calcutta, or when I was six years old and left my parents, aunties and uncles delirious with concern as I took a walk through a busy harbour and got lost.

Rock and our offspring are very tolerant of my little escapes into 'space'. They allow me the luxury of taking myself away once in a while to fathom things out and simply to 'be'. They often find my disappearances preferable to watching me pace the kitchen floor clutching my head in my hands. At least while I'm away they can eat their meals in the lounge and leave their empty plates on the floor. I can tell their goings on by the way they look flushed and out of breath on my return and by the soggy condition of the mop-head and the over-stacked dishwasher.

During that particular time away I did a lot of walking and allowed the sea air to soothe my grieving heart. It was early spring, before the tourist season, so I enjoyed long stretches of solitude. I went to Holywell Bay and trampled through course wild grass and climbed a steep sand bank. As I descended its sea facing decline and walked towards the water's edge I was suddenly struck by an absolute comprehension that God just is. In that moment time stopped and something beyond sight, sound or tangibility turned my rational thoughts inside out and upside down. I was thrown into a cornucopia of emotions. Excitement, shock, amazement, terror and awe had me fighting to regain my practical and logical thoughts lest I'd lost my senses. But that 'something' made its presence known and was both beyond and within me and I could not explain it away. It took a hold of me and convinced me that there really is something pretty huge at work in and around this universe.

I felt a bit silly after the encounter and looked around in embarrassment, wondering if I had acted strangely. Had I called out to the sea and sky? Had a passerby seen me fling my arms about or crouch down low in defence and wonder if I'd lost the plot? But I don't think I did anything weird, for my footprints in the sand indicated that I had stood quite still and my hands were warm in the pockets of my coat. I put the 'incident' down to grief. Maybe I was looking for a sign to let me know that my mother was alright, that she had found peace and was on her way to heaven. But the words that implanted themselves in my mind and reverberated around my head for a long time afterwards were not words of comfort or reassurance. On the contrary, they were words that challenged me and left me thinking, 'Hang on! I'm missing some vital point of life here. I'm seeing only a fraction of what it is really all about'. And so it was that I happened upon this journey. That was the moment that compounded my previous concerns and caused a volcanic eruption of questions to bubble up inside me. I became consumed with curiosity about the whole religious thing and the phenomenon of God.

I walked for miles that day and drank a few cups of coffee in cafés overlooking the sea as I tried to get my head round the incident. Previous 'experiences' of God that I'd had during acts of worship or prayer were nothing like that one. They would be better described as beautiful moments of elation and joy that filled my heart with warmth and love on sensing 'something other' within me. But that incident on the beach caused a major disturbance between my head and my heart. If that really had been an encounter with God, then how was I to relate or equate it with the God of the Bible? For the Bible is capable of throwing me into a stupor. I have often turned its pages and become utterly lost as to its intentions and have to confess that at times I have not been able to make head nor tail of what it is trying to say to me. The bloody battles and the terrifyingly judgemental God who points His finger at me makes me quiver with fear. I've tried to see the love involved in the act of sacrifice as God's only son is grotesquely murdered because I have sinned, but again I confess that it is a struggle. There are times when I want to slam shut the covers and shout, 'Enough, I say enough!'

Suddenly, my God of the beach was painting a totally different picture in my mind. Gone was the Old Father Time type figure that sits on a cloud and wags His finger at my antics below, and in his place appears energy of thought, an indescribable energy of knowledge with no visible form. The powerful sense that God 'just is' led me to reflect more deeply on *what* God is rather than *who* God is. I felt a presence of something that was not full of love but very love itself in pure undiluted form. It didn't speak to me or show itself to me. But in a way that I cannot understand or fathom I felt that it had thought and that it required thought in return from me. There is absolutely nothing that I can relate it to, no being and no gender, and yet it felt deeply worthy of my reverence.

So there I was, in desperate need of comfort from God but what I got instead was a challenge to search my soul, a challenge to delve. I had put a Bible into my suitcase with a view to looking up a few words of comfort, so I went back to the caravan where I was staying and spent a long evening looking at it through fresh eyes. If it was written in modern English as a story from beginning to end it could almost become a Disney tale about good versus evil. A happy ever after scenario can eventually be deduced in a strange sort of way. How much easier that would be to understand and accept, but no, instead I find that the Bible requires much study. I felt very tempted to put it on a shelf for the rest of my stay and simply rest assured in the knowledge that it was there. Instead I decided to look at it through fresh eyes upon a blank canvas and allow my imagination the free rein to run-amok through the books, chapters and verses.

For so long now the religious words and phrases that I have ritualistically repeated in church, often without glancing at the pages they are written on, have been said by me respectfully and prayerfully. They have given me comfort but there have also been times when I have looked around at the rest of the congregation and wondered if I am the only person there who has not grasped the full measure of their content. Although the sounds and pronunciations of the religious language are very familiar to me, many of their meanings have me scrambling through a fog of confusion. But suddenly something clicked over the next few days as I continued to read, and I felt a little like Dorothy in L. Frank Baum's book *The Wizard of Oz*. I was flown into a whole new world and just as Dorothy and Toto stumbled into new situations as they travelled the yellow brick road, bumping into new friends along the way, so did I. I came across ancient communities, cultures and tribes who are struggling to live in harmony with one another as battles for power and accumulation rage rampant.

I reflected on Moses and looked beyond the image of a bearded man dressed in a loin cloth brandishing a long stick as he wandered through dry sandy wilderness and found in his place a man of conscience and courage. I saw a man whose world was transformed when he came into spiritual collision with God. He could have kept the encounter to himself, I suppose, and continued to roam in solitary holy commune, but he didn't. He went on to turn things around in his own time and like a tumbling line of dominoes let loose the concept of one God that went on to turn the world upside-down with monotheistic religion.

Whether Moses' story is based on fact or myth mattered not much to me at that point but the meaning of the message did. It pointed to the restoring of values within communities to repent, or rather to turn around and become agreeable with one another. I looked at the laws, or commandments, that Moses discerned from God and saw all the, 'thou shalt' and 'thou shalt nots' in a different light. Those rules were totally applicable to the community being addressed amidst the context of their troubled situation; they made great sense. In order for a large band of people to move along together and to achieve their aim they had to live in accord with one another. They had to join in peaceful solidarity, and blaming each other over tiffs, partner swapping, stealing and killing each other was not likely to bring harmony to the group. Somehow Moses, as leader, had to come up with a plan of order that would control his mob. He went off on his own and prayed to his God for divine inspiration. During his solitude and close commune with God he discerned the laws that make as much sense to communities at large today as they did in his ancient times. God was to be seen as the point of unity between a disparaging motley crew of folk, God the unifying pinnacle of rock to steer and centre every member into a single spirit of accord. If every single member looked to that pinnacle of love to centre their aims they could all work together as one body in unity and treat each other on equal terms.

It all began to make sense to me, because whether or not each member of the group or tribe could feel, see or hear God personally was not really the point. The point was that they did have to believe that God, through their leader Moses, had their interests at heart. I don't suppose they felt, saw or heard much from the image of a god, the calf that they formed from melted gold, but what they did see in the image was something tangible to believe in and so keep their floundering hopes alive. What Moses managed to do through the power of his union with God was to draw the masses together. For while they were all leaning in different directions with no central meeting point to focus on, their unity fell apart, their trust dispersed. The tribal or community dream, to reach the 'promised land', had little chance of realisation without cohesion of purpose and spirit.

As fascinating and exciting as I am finding the Bible now to be, I cannot accept it as a recorded history of events to be taken literally; although following a visit to Luxor in Egypt I can gleam a picture of the plagues that may well have taken place there. As Rock and I cruised down the Nile on a boat and watched life taking place along its shores we saw frogs and insects aplenty. The mosquitoes that swarm above the water of the Nile have teeth like piranha fish that deliver a viciously aggravating poison into human flesh, and they particularly liked the taste of mine. They created sore and itchy lumpy blotches as reminders of their feast. I can readily comprehend how plagues of frogs and insects could have swarmed the land and caused catastrophic upset to the people. Many a scream arose from a bikini-clad beauty as a frog jumped onto her sun lounger. Each evening at the beautiful resort where we stayed classical music flowed gently through amplifiers just prior to sunset. On our first day Rock and I took a seat by the Nile and watched feluccas sail across the water as daylight dimmed. So lost were we in the serenity of the vision that we didn't notice others around us jump up and run for cover. A loud buzzing noise drowned out the sounds of music, as too did a fog of mist blur the sight of the vermillion setting sun. We gasped and choked as a man in traditional galapiya dress strolled along the edge of the Nile spewing out a forceful spray of insecticide from a canister he carried on his back. Our eyes stung fiercely as we coughed and panicked over the lethality of the potion but the operator, who wore no protective mask or clothing, continued to spray oblivious to the distress of tourists. I wonder if he is still alive. Combine the mischief of little living creatures with the unrelentingly hot sun and you can imagine a scene of plagues and an amount of physical discomfort that may result. I managed to swallow a germ that had me pleading for mercy for the following nine weeks.

We went to Luxor to satisfy Rock's fascination with ancient Egyptian history. My knowledge of Egyptology is limited, but after rising early in the mornings to explore the valleys of the great Kings and Queens my interest began to develop. I was fascinated by the ancient artwork that remains to portray vivid depictions of how life was during the times of the Pharaohs. I was struck by the lives of the workers, the masons, painters and decorators of the great tombs who lived a life of segregation lest they reveal the whereabouts of the treasure-filled royal tombs. A small cluster of primitive houses are still occupied by country families who live by the entrance to the remains of the workers' village. It is said that they reject all offers from the government to move into new accommodation as they prefer to live under a scorching sun on the west bank of the Nile and keep guard of their ancient secrets. An adorable little boy of about three years of age ran up to Rock and offered him a small home-made rag doll. Rock's heart was captured and he took the doll and gave the boy some money and some sweets, but within a second he was surrounded by children offering their wares. They clung to our heels in hope and we left them with our pockets empty.

I was particularly captivated by a stone carved statue of Akhenaten. The young ruler of apparent questionable sexual orientation had been a religious revolutionary in his reign. Was he simply crazy to revolt against the priests and set about an order to deface temples and destroy shrines to the pantheon of gods and go so far as to erase the most highly revered image of the Egyptian god Amun? Or did he have a life-changing encounter with one God who he found in the life giving sun 'Aten?' Was Akhenaten's God the same monotheistic God as encountered by Moses? Both men underwent transformation by 'something' out there and both were so moved by it that they acted upon it. Both appeared to interpret their God's power and intervention through acts of nature.

I found Egypt to be full of a wonder and mystery that arouses unquenchable thirst for discovery. As well as the nasty little germ that caused havoc with my tummy I also brought home a certain dissatisfaction surrounding the lack of spirituality in my life, from a land where many gods have been served. For Akhenaten's God Aten was rejected after his death, under the rule of his son Tutankhamun, who as a young boy was surely only acting on advice from threatened authorities. Back home in England I missed the magic that flows richly in the air under the middle-eastern sky. As I listened to the pealing ring of bells that rang out on a Sunday morning as I walked to church, I thought back to the haunting call from the mosque that had me stopping what I was doing to reflect in a moment of stillness and prayer. In the silence of a sunrise or sunset I found a sense of peace in the absence of the spray man.

I have a close and loyal friend who knows deep harmony with nature. He is an esteemed author and photographer of Worcestershire wildlife and is never happier than when he is trampling through the open green spaces with his dog. I have questioned him about his thoughts on an existence of God and wondered if he feels any sense of divine significance as he strolls in solitude through the countryside. As an evolutionist he studies the brutally harsh and natural acts of life and sure finality of death. I can see my friend's point when he says that no matter how much you look for divine presence or God, if you cannot feel it there is absolutely nothing that can convert you into believing it is there. He admits to thinking there may be 'something out there' because he has witnessed some strange happenings during the course of his life, but in the absence of personal intervention or inspiration it remains 'out there'.

It does cause me to ponder on the likelihood of there being a 'God shaped space in certain people's brains', for I returned home from Cornwall with yet another pressing query buzzing about my head. 'What am I to do and how am I to express the God that I met on the beach?' Because if I can no longer think of God as a man type figure watching over everybody, then how can I think of Jesus as being in heaven beside him? I was in a problematic place and all my comfortable images had come crumbling down around me. I lost sight of Jesus as an angelic looking man emanating bright golden hues and was left with not a single little lamb curled up by his feet. It was as if an artist had drawn his broad bristled brush across the canvas and erased all my comfort and security in one swift stroke. The world I had stumbled into was looking like a cold and lonely place and I felt as though I was standing on the edge of a great precipice.

There was a time in years gone by, during the college days of my youth, that when faced with a dilemma in my life I would blindly open the Bible and point my finger at the page. I took my guidance from the verse on which my finger landed. Often what was written there left me feeling riddled with guilt and remorse for my sinfulness. I would pray tearfully for forgiveness and make a promise to change my ways. If there was something that I particularly wanted but wasn't sure whether or not what I desired was good in the eyes of God, I would 'shape' the words of the verse to my favour. But as the Bible transformed before my eyes the pages between its covers have become less of a story incorporating lists of rules offering a code for living, and more of an invitation to eavesdrop on conversations between people who had encountered God and trusted in faith that God was real. Before I knew where I was or what I was doing I'd joined in and had begun to open up in self-awareness through conversation with the characters and God. I found that I'd stepped over the confusing metaphors and was enjoying an accompanied journey. I stopped pleading with God to give me a sign as I read, and by relinquishing the constraints of my human capacities to comprehend something so beyond my human comprehension I did begin to understand that I had to unleash God from my limitations. By listening in to the struggles of biblical characters and relating to their joys and their fears I found in the Bible an ongoing, and still relevant open-ended quest through the rituals of life. It occurred to me that the Bible has no ending, it doesn't finish on the last page but the very book itself is the beginning of a journey into faith. It is an invitation, an invitation to relax my boundaries of rational thought and make myself open to wonders, discernment and love on a higher plain. My own self-awareness increased as I read and I began to sense that I was not just being advised or expected to be 'good'. I was being invited to raise my levels of consciousness and take a look at what was going on around me. And yet even more than that I was beginning to see an invitation to focus on God and accept the responsibility of making my own way by reaching for my highest levels of self and world awareness in love. It's a scary invitation, but with only my feelings and experience to go on I have little choice but to take God in the faith and trust of my insights.

I've wondered where God is when I listen to the news and hear about appalling cases of cruelty, neglect and injustice. I've wondered what God is doing when people are suffering in pain and loneliness. I've wondered how God can simply watch countries go to war with one another and commit horrific crimes against humanity. I have shouted at God and asked, 'why do you let us make such a complete hash of this world, if you are so full of love why don't you stop us?' I pray and implore God to bring us peace on earth but nothing changes. It's just so easy to either blame or totally reject whatever concept of God I have ever held and deny any personal responsibility for evil and the shape of the world. But now I wonder, not what God is or is not doing but what we humans are doing and not doing. I wonder where our love is, and more troublesome and pressing, where is my love?

I can see now how dangerous it can be to extract a small portion of the Bible from its full context, and how damaging scenarios have been created by doing just that, and I feel naive in the extreme. The breaking down of the overall message, by taking a small fraction from the whole, could have and has had quite terrifying results for certain groups of people such as homosexual men and lesbian women, and given religion a very dirty name in the process. I can see how easily religion has caused harmful, oppressive conduct such as racism, the subordination of women and prejudices that lead to gross exclusivity, condemnation and evil destruction. The image of religion, I feel, is far removed from the spirituality of religion. My theology, as I look at the Bible, may be quirky and simple but one thing I am trying to learn is to stop worrying about getting everything 'right' in the eyes of those who I know are far more academic than me. Whatever my take on the Bible may be, the fact remains that it has awakened something deep within me and lifted me onto new heights of awareness. I'm beginning to turn my eyes away from the inner heavy weight of guilt that I insist on carting around and look further afield, beyond myself, to the challenges that face us all. Something is changing and my identity is shifting. My Dad's mission, as opposed to his job description which forced my role upon me, is lighting up my path. Through my explorations and experience of God I am beginning to really understand what his life was about and my respect for him is rocketing to yet new heights.

While I am getting to grips with a personal understanding of God and while I have tremendous respect for Sigmund Freud and his great observations, I no longer feel discomforted by his suggestion that I may be seeing my biological father as my God. But I do have a little niggle about referring to or addressing God as Father, because as soon as I do the image of a male figure appears in my mind's eye faster than I can blink it away. It's like telling me not to think of a pink elephant or a purple frog but the deed is done before I can take control. I would like to say that my search is over but that would be like saying, after a back-breaking weekend tidying up the garden, that it is done, I have finished. My garden never lies dormant or stops growing. I may have sorted it for a little while but soon new seeds and weeds will rise up from the ground and force me to decide what to nurture and what to pluck out and discard. So, as close as I am getting, I'm still, as yet, nowhere near home.

SOUTHALL

It was while I was still alone in Cornwall that I turned my close attention to my long term childhood friend, Jesus, Jesus of gentle, meek and mild disposition who loved and befriended all. But do you know, it's a funny thing that I cannot find the man who fits this description, and especially not one sporting long blond hair and blue eyes, in my Bible. I'm not intending to sound facetious at all here because I thought I had grown out of that childhood image but, I realise with a bit of a shock, perhaps not fully.

As I walked along Newquay's main shopping street, trying to avert my eyes from the golden baked Cornish pasties in the baker's window and shift them instead to the colourful display of fruits on the grocer's stand, I recalled the sight of my Dad as he preached from a pulpit. His face was not wreathed in pious smiles, it had an expression of earnest plea that invited his congregation to think about what Jesus was intending when he angrily turned the trading tables in the temple. I held onto that word, anger, as I walked down to the beach with my paper bag of apples and cherries.

If God is love, then surely love feels and longs, knows and comprehends and suffers alongside suffering. How then could such pure intense love send a part of itself, its child with a mind of its own to think and feel for its own self, to suffer such horrors as crucifixion? Suddenly the fruits tasted sour on my tongue and even the waft of fish and chips could not reawaken my appetite.

The God that made such an impact on me also fuelled me with dilemmas. As a Christian I am bound to assert the claim that Jesus Christ is the only son of God who was conceived by the Holy Spirit and born of the Virgin Mary. And furthermore, that he was crucified, he died and then rose back to life on the third day. Why, I wondered with a feeling of dread descending upon me, did I have to bring that assertion into question? That was the point that had me looking out at a cold and lonely world from the edge of a precipice.

*

Southall in Middlesex was once a small agricultural community housing fewer than seven hundred people, perhaps something akin to Cold Hesleden. In the early eighteen hundreds cows and sheep grazed lazily in green fields and the locals earned their living by working crops of wheat and barley. During this era an act of humanity took place in the Middlesex County Asylum in Southall where, as a self-supporting community, the inmates were taught trade skills and learnt crafts. As it became apparent that such sensitive treatment enriched and inspired the lives of patients the next superintendent to take over ended the practice of making inmates wear chains of restraint. An honourable and liberating claim to fame for Southall, I would say.

Jim often found himself in precarious situations. I've

watched on in horror as he's climbed onto church roofs to repair disjointed tiles or seal a leaking gutter. But one Sunday afternoon he came home from the very same mental health institution which had been renamed as Saint Bernard's Hospital, with bruises around his neck. As a part-time chaplain he took an active responsibility towards the nurturing of patients' wellbeing and led regular Sunday services in their chapel. On this particular occasion he felt a presence behind him as he placed hymn books on a table near the entrance. He turned around to find his eyes level with a very tall man's broad chest. He greeted the man in welcome and smiled his pleasure at seeing him again, for he was a regular attendee. But on this Sunday his medication had not reacted to keep his condition on an even keel.

'I am God'. The man's deep voice boomed and resounded around the old building.

'And I am very pleased to meet you'. Jim responded.

'I am God', the man repeated slowly and deliberately.

'I am Jim', he replied, and so it went on in such manner until the man cupped his large hands around Jim's head and lifted him clean off the floor.

'I have come to bless you', he continued, but Jim could not reply because his mouth was clamped firmly shut against the man's thumbs. Jim willed someone, anyone, to enter the chapel and rescue him as he was carried the full length of the aisle towards the large cross that hung from the wall behind the altar. He could have fought the man off but was not prepared to further distress an unbalanced state of mind. Jim got a very uncanny feeling as he was lowered to the ground. As his feet landed gently on the floor the man pulled Jim's arms and stretched them wide horizontally to fit the shape of the cross. Panic began to rise somewhat in his chest as the man put his hands in his pocket as though feeling for something, and Jim thought that something might just happen to be a hammer and some nails. Luckily for him the door burst open and two doctors in search of their missing patient entered in the nick of time to gently steer the man away, leaving Jim to rub his painful neck and face.

He laughed about the episode as he recalled it, or at least he laughed at himself and how he must have looked had anyone been there to witness his role in the scene. Mostly he was greatly saddened by the fragility of the minds of the people who had little choice but to reside in that hospital. He worked in group therapy sessions with alcoholics and among other groups of people who were dependent on drugs. I can remember him telling me how he cried on two occasions, once when he watched a man walk along a long corridor as though he carried the weight of the entire world's trouble on his back. And again during a music therapy session when a woman who suffered from depression smiled for the first time in many years as she struck a note on a metal triangle and rejoiced at its tinkling tone.

I have often marvelled at the varied scope of projects that Jim involved himself in, such as the persuading of legal experts to offer their services free of charge to people of many faiths who struggled to find their way in our foreign land. His role as chairman of Victim Support groups, both during his working life and in retirement, led him to reach out a caring hand to victims of crime. He was always putting his full-throttled energies into supporting people in need, most often to those on the fringes of life. I have always admired and respected his devotion to helping others, but often it was misunderstood by some who thought he should stick to his role in the Church. It has been through getting to know Jesus in a new light that I have fully been able to understand and reconcile my Dad's visions and missions with his call to be a minister of the Methodist Church. I can now distinguish how his zeal, that never did outrun his love and compassion for all human beings, was in tune with the life and acts of love that Jesus, the Christ of Christianity whom Jim vowed to serve, himself performed.

Rock and I paid a visit to Southall as we often do when our supply of Indian spices runs low. We parked the car on the street where I lived, close to the house that was my home for many years. A walk through the park brought a smile to my face as we passed benches set into concrete platforms in a formation designed to encourage conversation. There on summer days, groups of Indian men, some with turbans and some without, sit and commune with one another enjoying friendly banter and setting a lovely scene. I couldn't help but wonder what type of group such a setting would invite in some other districts, and I felt sad and guilty as I pictured groups of aggressive youths, young people perhaps alienated and isolated through neglect, with nowhere else to go, possibly drawing up plans to cause harm either in revenge or self defence against opposing gangs. I watched red double-decker buses transporting people along the main road and remembered many times when I sat on the upper deck on my way to the tube station. I could be on Oxford Street within an hour to spend an afternoon in mother-daughter companionship, or with friends to shop, or even to eat beetroot sandwiches with my Dad after the business of the day had been attended to.

On this day's visit Rock and I lunched in the Shahi-nan-kebab house, the nearest equivalent to a stand selling Indian street food to passersby. We peered into the windows of shops selling richly ornate jewels and browsed arcades displaying rolls and folds of beautiful fabrics to be wrapped around the body as a sari. We explored shops selling everything from cans of pop to toys, kitchenware, hair oils and televisions, and bought unpackaged fruit in the market for a fraction of supermarket prices and ate them out of a brown paper bag. A soothing smell of incense wafted through the town mingled with a delicious aroma of freshly cooked curry from cafés and restaurants. I loved living in this place and remembered how I had pined for it when I went away to college.

Towards the end of the day we came out of an Asian supermarket laden with ingredients to make authentic Bengali curries and then walked along South Road to stand and rest our eyes on my old church. I put my heavy bags down on the pavement and feasted my eyes upon the familiar building. Rock and I smiled at one another affectionately in remembrance of the day on which we had stood outside the front doors to pose for our wedding photographs. Our photographer didn't suggest we adoringly gaze into one another's eyes in front of rose bushes, for there were none nearby. Instead he dodged between the London buses on the busy and noisy road and snapped his shutter when he could. Our photographs were framed at the edges with women passing by dressed in salwar kameez as they carried children and shopping bags to and from town.

Naturally I thought about my Dad as I looked at Kings Hall Methodist Church. I laughed as I remembered him in his overalls climbing onto the high roof or working in the boiler room, his hands covered in grease as he sparked the temperamental contraption into action. He saved hundreds of pounds by seeing to maintenance jobs himself rather than calling someone in who would hand over a hefty invoice. Not far away stands the Sikh Gurdwara and I thought of the times that I went inside with Jim. We would take off our shoes and cover our heads with scarves before going into the hall of worship. As we entered we'd walk to the high platform under a golden canopy and lower ourselves to our knees before bowing low in front of the Guru Granth Sahib, the holy book. Then I would take a place with the women and sit cross-legged on the floor so as not to point my feet at the holy book and Dad would do the same with the men. Even though I couldn't understand the language being spoken I always loved the ceremony, reverence and sense of serenity that I found there.

Jim was passionate about unity and equality. He worked hard to form harmonious relations amongst the different faiths in Southall and in order to interact effectively he expanded his knowledge of languages by learning Urdu and Guajarati. Because he was so firmly grounded in his own faith and beliefs in Christianity he was able to be freely open to the faiths of others. Just as he did when he lived and worked in India, he aimed and worked tirelessly towards the sharing of faiths in an effort to sustain a loving community living together as one. He loved Southall and all it represented very deeply. That's why, as I took a last look at Kings Hall before setting off back through the park to our car, I felt a lump come into my throat. I recalled the scene of the night when my Dad had leapt over the wall of our front garden and banged furiously upon the door for us to let him in. When Mum opened the door she let out a loud cry upon seeing the blood that rushed from an open gash on her husband's forehead. A gash caused by the truncheon of a policeman on horseback.

Gradually the town of Southall grew, mainly through developments in transport, with the Grand Junction Canal linking London to the Midlands via Southall, and later as the Great Western Railway Company opened a line which included a station and drop-off point there. As industry replaced agriculture people moved into the area in search of work. Many of the first to arrive were Welsh migrants who filled the air with their tuneful accents, followed by South Asians from India and Pakistan who, it is reputed, were invited to come and work in a local factory owned by a former British Indian Army Officer. Gradually, as work prospects enlarged with the London transport system and opportunities for work arose at nearby Heathrow Airport, more Asians crossed the seas to England and settled in Southall. It became a multicultural community where members of the Hindu, Muslim, Christian and, more predominantly, Sikh faiths lived harmoniously together. In the 1970s that untroubled community came under uninvited assault.

During the run up to the general election of 1979, only three years after a young seventeen-year-old boy of the Sikh faith had been stabbed to death by a gang who were inspired by the National Front Party, that very same party opted to hold their election meeting in Southall. They had no supporters within the community but, and here I only presume, they desired an opportunity to stir up trouble and conflict. Once news got out about the meeting it spread through the angry and insulted community like wildfire. Many racist riots were taking place around the country during this time, so I fail to understand why permission was granted for such a meeting to take place other than for the sake of serious mischief.

The day before the meeting was due to take place, five thousand people congregated and peacefully marched to Ealing town hall in protest. A petition signed by ten thousand residents was handed over, but to no effect. The twenty-third day of April, Saint George's day, saw a bus load of National Front members pull up outside Southall town hall and enter the building under protection from the Metropolitan Special Patrol Group. As they walked from the bus to the steps of the town hall, members of the party stuck up their fingers in 'V' signs. Such stirring up of the situation incited violent reaction and naturally, under such provocation some of the young Asians flew towards them, but the police intervened by fighting them back.

After much careful consideration and planning with other leading members of the community little Jimmy rolled up his sleeves on that day to take his position as one of the front men in non-violent protest. Shops and factories closed their doors to business at one o'clock in the afternoon to join together in a show of unity. Jim fronted a mass of community members as they linked arms in peaceful solidarity. At this point I am deeply reluctant to replay the controversial actions of the police and dredge up old conflicts that I feel are best left where I hope they will remain, in the past. But it has to be said that a nasty blood bath was the outcome of the day, resulting in the death of an anti-racist young man named Blair Peach. Many other injuries were sustained by men and women as the riot erupted. Media coverage in the aftermath portrayed the scene of mixed-race anti-racists acting like violent aggressive thugs. Such headlines of misrepresentation did nothing, in my opinion, to support the injured community or depict how they had been treated by racist agitators and the police force alike. The terrifying noise that rolled through the town that afternoon, as the police drummed their riot shields with truncheons, echoed in the frightened ears of residents, and Jim, for a long time afterwards. Streams of blood that ran through the streets of Southall got washed away by a torrential downpour of rain that added to the grimness of that day. The mark of hurt took a while to heal.

I took it as a matter of course that my Dad often lived life on the edge. He was never a man to stay quiet if he thought words needed to be said to turn a problem around. And believe me, as his daughter I have been on the receiving end and know this to be true. He has been accused of interfering in politics at times and told to stay within the boundaries of the Church and religion. But he simply could not sit by and do nothing if he thought injustice was being done; he was a man who acted, always non-violently, and in so doing he made enemies within certain groups in churches along the way. I know that my Dad was a deep thinker and that he was full of compassion and love and I know that he kept close commune with God and never acted on anything without basing his motives in love and prayer. To quote the words of my brother Timu, *'There is no doubt that our Dad was a spiritual man whose Christian faith was at his centre'.*

It is with those memories replaying through my mind and with Timu's words about our father ringing in my ears that I find the courage to display my new-found faith in a fully human Jesus. As the sour taste of cherries stained my tongue in Cornwall I faced a heavy choice, I could continue to live with past images and so not ruffle my old religious feathers. Or I could make the decision to abandon fear, release my shackles and become my own person by admitting that in the human figure of Jesus I have found liberation and freedom. My flagging spirit has been awakened.

DIVINE RESPECT

I went through a period of gloom following my elation and liberation in Jesus. On my last morning in Cornwall I walked along the beach at Newquay and searched for a smooth flat stone. When I found one I stood close to the water's edge and skimmed it into the sea just as my Dad had taught me to do. It bounced four times and I was pleased. I walked from the harbour along the exposed path of the headland and passed the imposing hotel that reminds me of a haunted tower, and I questioned how I was going to deal with my new findings from there on. Jim was a very down-to-earth man who made it his duty to discover the workings of everything he came into contact with. I feel sure that he went through similar searches to my own but, alas, I find no record of his conclusions other than the way he led his life. How did he see Jesus, was it his divinity or his humanity that challenged Jim to a life of preaching the good news? What did he think about the resurrection of Jesus?

    I found a pleasant niche, sheltered from the winds, to sit on the pale sands of Fistral beach. I watched surfers ride the waves and plunge into the icy cold salty water and shivered at the prospect. I thought of numerous jokes that have been told about Jesus walking on water and I wondered what he would make of surf boards. I liked to think that he'd probably have a go and balance himself quite well. Just thinking that thought renewed my sense of liberation because years ago I would not have dared to put Jesus in the same frame as a joke lest I incur the wrath of God.

As I continued to review my interpretations of the Holy texts I could not help but think that such a supernatural concept as the miraculous birth and the resurrection of the dead almost detracts from the real miracle that was Jesus' life. If God wanted to shake up the ways of the world and draw everybody to the power of divine love, why choose such a subtle way of going about it? Why create an obscure being and have him born as a lowly peasant in the back of the beyond, why not have him born into a position of power? But then who am I to raise such a question, as clearly Jesus was the right man for the job because his name is familiar all over the world, all these years on, and his life did indeed bring about change. Was that because he was conceived by the Holy Spirit? Or was it because he was a man who drew so close to God that he was able to discern the very will of God's love for all human kind? Was Jesus so in tune with God's will that he became one with God's nature, *he in God and God in him,* so to speak?

As I stood up and brushed the sand from my jeans and made my way back to my parked car I shivered. How was I going to go back to church feeling this way? I'd not been for a while anyway since my mother's death and had not been able to attend during her months of incapacity and, if the truth be known, I still had a little upset inside me because I felt that the church had neglected her during her confinement. As I got into my car I felt the sharp pain of loss fill my heart. I missed my parents. I wanted my Dad's guidance and I wanted his approval for where my beliefs were leading me, but he is gone and I'm left to work it all out for myself. I reminded myself about the invitation I discerned from the Bible to focus on God and accept the responsibility of making my own way by reaching for my highest levels of self and world awareness in love. As a mother of grown children, there I was needing my own Dad to assure me of his approval because the thought of distorting all that he held dear and lived by tore at my heart. But as I took a final look at the deep blue foaming sea I caught a glimpse of him. I saw the real man of mischief that was my Dad and somehow I thought that if he were still alive he would be rejoicing in my search and laughing on the edge of his seat, rubbing his hands together with an eager sparkle in his eyes, calling to me, 'Come on kid, keep going, keep going, don't give up'.

*

The word 'sin' causes me to squirm and brings about a desire to curl up into a tight ball and rock to and fro in a state of self-disgust and unworthiness. Or, at least, it used to. Recently, I walked the length of the small town where I live and I recalled the flourishing community it used to be. The high street was once a hive of activity every Saturday as people flocked to shop and meander in the sure hope of bumping into a friend or two. Groups of people gathered to chat and enjoy a sense of belonging. Now it often stands almost empty with many of its shops closed down and little laughter to energise its air. The only sound I heard was the voice of a man shouting loudly as he stood before a poster that he'd pinned to a wooden board. He was calling to the few people who walked past him without acknowledgement to turn from their sins towards Jesus and be saved.

As I thought about the high street I questioned whether one of the sins of the community and nation is the way that we have deprived our towns and side roads of shared laughter and tears. Have we communities sinned against ourselves by allowing huge corporations to seduce us into shopping for everything under one roof at cheaper prices than a sole trader can possibly afford to offer? When Rock and I first moved onto the street where we live we had a post office, two small grocery stores, an off-licence, a newsagent, a bakery and a hardware store. Every day people paused at the post office to natter and have their say about whatever was on their minds before crossing the road to buy freshly baked bread and talk some more. For some it was the only chance they had to meet with others before going back to their homes alone. Now we have only a newsagent's shop and I rarely see my neighbours unless they are getting in or out of their cars. It makes me question and re-evaluate the concept of sin and the need for forgiveness.

It looks to me more like a case of human beings battling for accumulation and power than God turning a blind eye to the needs and prayers of a society. The man's voice that rang through the high street fell, unsurprisingly, on deaf ears as he told how Jesus could save. I felt that sadly he spouted jargon that neither inspired nor invited the turning around of ways. His message eluded all reference to the saving powers of holistic, social, economic and ethical health that hold a promise of communal salvation. The town where I live consists mainly of white middle-class people and as yet is not home to people of many different faiths. Also as yet, thankfully, gang warfare and knife stabbings do not hold centre stage, but in places where such crimes divide communities, social health cries out for salvation, the very sort of national dis-ease that Jesus confronted. Issues of a political and religious nature that I think Jesus set out to bring into a state of health, issues that divided and unleashed injustice, oppression and inequality within the society of his time. Perhaps Jesus was pointing towards individual wholeness and communal health.

Niggling doubts as to the origins of Jesus taunt me, and yet at the same time does it really matter how he came to be or is the importance of what he did more relevant? For me the depth of love that he poured out in vast quantities, at great personal risk, outweighs my need for proof of conception and in that frame I have to accept that I become open and vulnerable to much criticism. I imagined the scene of a passionate young man in the prime of his life who took his Jewish faith very seriously. I saw a man who was brought up in a rural village and worked alongside his brothers in the family business. I can imagine him watching his Dad intently as he taught him the tricks of the stone mason, or carpentry trade. An ordinary boy but one who, along with his peers, possibly witnessed horrors going on around him as his homeland suffered under harsh political rule following the Roman invasion. My mind created an image of Jesus as a strong silent type who spent a lot of time in thought as he worked. Maybe he wondered why such long established rules of tradition dominated his religion and maybe he even thought that some of them got in the way of union with God. Maybe he struggled to reconcile the teachings of the priests, as he attended worship, with what he saw going on around him in a society at odds with one another under a ruling empire that included authority from the Church but also demanded allegiance to the rule from the Church.

I can never be sure of the facts surrounding Jesus'

conception but it helps me a little to remember that during those years the mysteries of female ovaries had not yet been discovered. It was understood that the ready fertilised egg, the seed, was implanted into a women's womb during an act of sexual intercourse by the man, the sole maker of babies. For me perhaps the miracle of the birth was more that Joseph stood by Mary and saved her reputation and possibly her life as, according to the laws, she could have been stoned to death for being with child before marriage. Maybe she had an affair, maybe she was raped or even maybe Joseph, with Mary's consent, was unable to restrain his virility. I will simply never know the truth any more than I can refrain from asking the questions. But what I do know is that the life and ministry of Jesus calls me to review my relationship with and my expression of God as I accept personal responsibilities towards others with whom I share this world.

With my sheltering images vanishing and the edge of my precipice crumbling to a frighteningly narrow ledge I turn my attention to God as a comforter. Can I find comfort in God that I now claim to be the very source and essence of love and God that I feel is in everything everywhere? I do still have a friend in Jesus but not the sort of friend who is going to stroke my brow till I drop off to sleep and keep me safe until morning time. I cannot simply lay things down to God's will when I don't understand them or when I seek comfort amongst adversities. I believe that the time we have on this earth, the time between our births and our deaths are vital years in which we face joys, fears and pains and aim to do the best we can for each other out of compassion and love. If we are to have free will, and if God is pure undiluted love that does not insist on its own way, and so grants that free will to us, then I feel that we are called to make the best of situations that are thrust upon us or that we choose, rightly or wrongly to walk headlong into.

I get confused when I hear people say that it must have been God's will when something awful has happened. I don't really understand why God would allow a tragedy to take place for the purpose of bringing about something helpful for another situation or person. I can see where the idea might spring from if someone suffers a dreadful illness or accident and through their experience they put all their energies into helping other people or situations, but I still struggle to take such incidents as being God's will. Rather I see God as the very source of love that wills love into every one of us, and if we can accept and live that love then change and transformation has the freedom to occur. It somehow now seems strange to me that I should lay claim to an acceptance of God's will or refer to God's hand and involvement in acts that I just simply do not have an answer for. Why would God, for instance, decide that it was OK for my parents' twin boys to die? Surely, a God that is love would not intend that their deaths happen in order to bring about something good but would instead suffer alongside the bereaved and breathe a spirit of love, blessings and hope upon them and will them to survive the loss and keep going forward in love and hope, rather than cease to live in a cloud of bitterness.

Perhaps our creation by God can be interpreted as us having been born with love in the image of God's love, and with conscious thought in the image of God's that has the power to obtain knowledge, rather than we having been literally formed by God into human beings. In God our capacity to love and our capacity for knowledge and awareness have room to flourish and be nurtured ever increasingly. I'm perceiving creation as an ongoing, ever transforming gift of love to life that continues to create life in greater fullness of love as our self awareness and insight deepens, as opposed to one singular act of creation at the beginning of all time. I am fascinated by Darwin's theory of evolution and see evolvement of the species by natural selection in the light of natural universal wonder and mystery, of which I see God as at the centre. Is survival of the fittest amongst wildlife so very different from the emotional tactics we humans apply to life? But because we have the capacity to love and we have knowledge, we are surely brought into questions of conscience as to how we survive and live alongside one another.

I have had to face the fact that I may be destroying the notion of Jesus being God's gift of love to life as well as the notion of God's gift of sacrifice by bringing Jesus down to human level. But in the way that I view creation I see Jesus and his ministry as a transforming, love and life enriching act of new creation in itself. A creation willed by God's love and delivered by Jesus' love and acceptance to the call. My journey has proved at times to be a sojourn along a desperately lonely road. I have touched mountain tops of sheer joy in God and I have plunged to the bottom of valleys of darkness in doubt and despair. I have longed for this particular stretch of the journey, the journey into God, to end and have been very tempted to jump off before the next hurdle. But I cannot because 'something' will not let me. When I began to settle in my persistent thoughts that Jesus may after all be only human, I crossed a boundary and felt as though I had been stripped naked in a crowded place. I felt vulnerable and lost, for I'd crossed a lonely divide and could no longer turn back. I asked myself, am I rocking the tenets of the Christian faith that my parents lived by and that to this point, however superficially, I have lived by too? I have embarked upon this book and now wonder if I have the strength and courage to complete it.

I'm in a lonely place at this moment, my head is full of confusion, I feel vulnerable, shaky and want to scream aloud for clarity. Many tears threaten to fall but what good would they do? I have felt God, I do feel God and I see a life-changing message in Jesus, Jesus the revolutionary boundary breaker who dared to confront the authorities. I would hazard a guess that he was a man with charisma and a huge magnetic aura that attracted people to him, but a man of humility and great compassion who put his own interests aside. I don't think his intention was to create a new religion but rather to revive the Jewish faith by applying it to his present time. Similarly, I don't see that he desired to be personally worshipped and obeyed but rather to breathe fresh new life into his religion. I'm seeing in Jesus a man who experienced God at a mighty rich level and exuded God's spirit of love. A man who had experienced God's love so profoundly that he carried the presence of God within him and people who got close to him experienced the presence of God through him. So in Jesus, God and God's nature of compassion was actually present in human form acting and moving on earth. And that, I see as God's gift of love to life and that is the divine respect I have for Jesus.

It's what Jesus did in the power of God's love that fills me with incredulity. The bravery of the man astounds me. I did go back to church a few months after I got home from Cornwall. I didn't find it easy in many ways, one of which being that I choked up with every hymn that was played. I could hear their voices, Mum's eager, tuneful delight in the words that she sang and Dad's rich bass vocals that added depth to the overall delivery of the hymn. But I did find that my anger subsided in the welcoming warmth of friendship and I could understand that perhaps people hadn't knowingly neglected to show love to my mum but were just caught up in the business and orderliness of life. We are all, after all, only human; and yet if Jesus too was only human he must have had immeasurable depths of love and compassion to continue with his mission even to the point of death. For had he dropped his cause and fled he could have saved his life but nothing would have been achieved; instead, in order to achieve he was prepared to face the cross. Did Jesus turn the tables in the temple for political reasons? Was he so aggrieved by the empire and the way in which the Church was bowing down to its rule and serving it before God? Was this the reason that he got so angry and lost it? I think perhaps it was. I also think that his anger was not fuelled by foul temper but soaked in compassion, born from frustration that the Church was blinkered to the real needs of what was taking place around it.

I see Jesus as a revolutionary. As one who fronted a non-violent revolution against the system, taking great care along the way never to be misunderstood as one who wanted any part in military warfare or hatred. He acted on behalf of people at the very edge of existence, social outcasts who knew oppression, poverty and sheer neglect. People like those we see living in cardboard boxes on England's streets, people like Praem Chand in Titigarh and people who spew and get spewed upon because of the colour of their skin or the faith that they live by. He acted to lift women from their undervalued status and rocked many boats and upset many apple carts in the process. His message, his good news, was to encourage people to turn back to God and live and work in love, to see God as Lord of all hearts and so create heaven on earth with God as the sovereign ruler. But,

I suppose instead he was seen to be a troubling upstart who challenged the system and threatened the establishment with his talk of kingdoms. He was a man who had to die.

Rock and I went to the Vatican in Rome to see the Pope, not a personal sitting of course, but just to get a feel for the place. We did manage to get a glimpse of him dressed in his white finery some way in the distance, but the clearer view came from the many big screens that stood at intervals, showing a close-up of his figure. It felt a little as though we were at a concert as people around us gasped in awe as though he were a celebrity. Our well travelled daughter was with us and told us about a place in the city where the steps, reputed to be the ones that Jesus carried his cross up on the way to his crucifixion, had been reinstalled. We set off to find the steps and when we could not we decided to ask one of the multitude of priests that we passed to guide us in the right direction.

We made it to Santa Scala just in time before the doors were locked for the day and went inside the former papal palace, opposite the Basilica of Saint John Lateran. The building that contained the white marble steps encased in wood for protection, brought to Rome from Jerusalem in the fourth century AD, held an air of deep reverence. We were invited to climb the twenty-eight deeply worn steps, not on our feet but on our knees. I have no idea if Jesus carried his cross up those steps or indeed if his feet ever touched them but as I climbed them, painfully and laboriously, I cried heartfelt tears for all that man tried to achieve and for how his life ended. I looked at my daughter and a photograph of my son that I carried in my purse and cried again for Jesus' Mother Mary. How on earth does a woman cope with the death of her child under any circumstances, and how utterly wretched must it have been for Mary the woman as she watched her son die an agonising and humiliating tragic death? For however she conceived her son she did indeed carry him and give birth to him and her pain must have been immense.

Mary must have felt desperate at times as her son began to rattle the security of their family life. I thought of what Lizzie, little Jimmy's mother went through when her son first announced his intention to become a Methodist minister and invited ridicule upon himself, being an uneducated pit lad. Lizzie was always very conscious of what other people might think and lived her life privately so as not to attract attention. But then her son goes and throws her into the limelight and she had no choice but to get on with it. Worse still, her son then tells of his decision to leave the country and go to a place so far away that she would have to endure years without even seeing his face. Lizzie at least had pride in her son's work and title to uphold her, but Mary must have been nearly crazy with worry about the spectacle her son was making of himself before the authorities. Jesus not only ceased to bring in money from his work but created havoc within his community and generational family line, as stigma was heaped upon them by his actions.

I have focused all my thoughts on God and centred on God as my pinnacle of rock that guides me. But what of people like my wildlife expert friend, who feels no sense of God yet knows compassion and love for all creatures, both human and wild that have life? I come back to my predicament of Jesus as being the only way to God. How do we define what or who God is to us? The more I think and puzzle over the mysteries of God and the Christian religion the more my brain curdles. I have accepted the ethos of the resurrection even by accepting Jesus as a human being, because even though he died his message lives on and his life has had purpose and brought goodness. In that respect he continues to live and turn things around for people and situations that take his mission and his message to heart. But is he the only gateway to God?

The underlying message of most religions is to have love and compassion for one another. Jesus underlined the importance of doing only to another that which you would have done to yourself. We have to give love and compassion with sincerity of spirit, in order to receive love and compassion in return. Giving what we hope to receive is a universal offering that could shape a more harmonious world void of greed and hatred. If religions steer us towards the same goal of love and compassion regardless of the gateway to God or a higher supreme being that we centre on, does it matter that they are different and travel by a different route? We are all in this together whether we like it or not. For the duration of our time on earth we share the same space and it's really not that big a space anymore; our world grows smaller all the time as the wonders of technology evolve to connect nations from shore to shore, with each country's economic survival depending on another's.

I have, and will continue to explore and study books written by theologians, religious philosophers and scientists in my quest. I have even implored atheistic scientists to convince me that there is no God, but it cannot be done, any more than I can convince another person that my God of the beach is real. The powerful energy that interacted with my own that day transformed the way that I think and feel and love, and the spirit of that energy continues to live within me. But it does not control me. Rather it inspires me to take control of myself and in reverence to its almighty transformational power lovingly honour all that I meet on my journey through life and show tolerance and respect for the journey of others. I strive to live in the spirit of God and in the spirit of love that is not ours to hold onto but to be shared as naturally as we breathe in and out. The life of Jesus helps me to comprehend the importance of circulating love, humility and patience and, perhaps above all else, compassion. It is not an easy life to emulate and I'm beginning to understand what Jesus meant by entering through the narrow gate. I don't think he guards that gateway to God against other faiths that don't look to him as the key. But instead he perhaps hopes that loving actions such as his may be mirrored by all human beings in an effort to shed destructive and negative attitudes that cause harm and separation.

From my own experiences I have learnt that the real dangers of religions occur when dogma outweighs spirituality. If we abide by rules and traditions that we do not fully understand and make them our god, we run the risk of being burdened by guilt and creating negative energies that dominate and criticise others who see things differently to ourselves. Conflicts begin to mingle in the air that surrounds us and breed more powerfully than acceptance. My personal views are that all religions which encourage loving, compassionate acceptance and tolerance are helpful to all of life. But spirituality and respect must shine through.

I feel content with where I now stand in my beliefs, but I am no angel and will have to spend the rest of my days in the ongoing practice of real loving. When I go wrong I will make the choice, not to put on my hair shirt but to recognise the error of my ways and make an attempt to turn around and away from all thoughts that have the potential to cause harm or create negativity. Perhaps I have strayed and sidestepped the path of what I once considered the doctrines of Christianity to be, I don't know. My intention is not to decry in the least the message of the religion which I still choose to follow because of the example of Jesus. But from this leg of the journey, as I look at things a little differently, I will have to discern my way forward in the Church and look to pay honour and reverence in a way that sits comfortably and expresses my experience of God. I want to dissolve my barriers, formed from fears of 'getting things wrong' in the light of theologies and doctrines, and step forward in hope.

Surely there has to be a solution to the problem of 'faith battle'. How can any of us truly know that we have got it right? How can anything be right or helpful to harmonious living if it breeds contempt and creates barriers? My concern is, that as long as we each insist on ownership of 'the truth', whether it be through our chosen faith or atheism, we are expounding vital energies on arguments and proof instead of seeking to find a way of sharing in a loving oneness of spirit and unity in the world. Healthy disagreements can be fun, inspiring and liberating if aired in a spirit of tolerance. There seems to be but a mere thread between love and hate and I wonder how much strength it gains from fear to keep it in place. When Rock and I went to India we encountered fear within ourselves, fear of the unknown and the fear of stepping outside our personal comfort zones. It was not an emotion I had expected to feel as I revisited the land of my childhood, but it just goes to show how readily we human beings entrap ourselves in cages of familiarity and tradition.

A FRETFUL FLIGHT

So far I have discovered, over many hours spent in record offices and on the internet, that the majority of my ancestors were practical people who earned their living by working with their hands. As pit men and women I can deduce that they were grafters and not shy of hard work; none, it appears, were financially wealthy. Many of them were gifted, with creative natures, and a thread of wood-carving and dressmaking has woven its way down through the generations and continues to do so. In general, it appears, they were a happy bunch who thrived on close community spirit and loving friendships and, despite the odd scandal born of lust, I've unearthed no signs of falling out with one another. I feel proud and content with my lineage.

Delving into my roots has had me travelling around England re-visiting the places of my own childhood as well as those of my parents and grandparents, in search of that elusive place that I can call home. Jimmy and Irene, no matter where they resided at the time, always referred to Blackhall as home, and I've always wanted a place that I too can call home, a place that signifies stability, a welcoming place to which I can return to recharge my batteries and glory in the satisfaction that at some point in my life I belonged there. I went to Yorkshire to take a look at the huge, double-fronted Victorian house with its cold, dark, cobweb filled cellar that Timu used to delight in locking me in alone, but I had a very loud scream which always resulted in him getting told off. The cobbled back street where we used to play was full of new children playing their own games and I couldn't help but smile as I noticed that most of the children were of Indian origin, I think my Dad, Jim, would have enjoyed the scene. Just as we moved into this house on our return from India, new generations of Indians are now living and sleeping, perhaps even in the once pink and blue decorated bedroom that I shared with my doll Rosebud. Or maybe they play in the green painted room where Timu and Jim built an impressive railway layout from papier-mâché and guided their electric trains over mountains, down into valleys, through tunnels, under bridges and across rivers.

I walked the familiar route to my junior school and yet still I felt a sickening dread in the pit of my stomach. The sight of the old building and the playground made me tremble so I decided to just leave it behind where it belonged, in the past, and made my way, instead, to a place where I had always found joy. I drove to Haworth, home of the Brontës and walked through the cemetery, where I was dismayed to find that Emily Brontë, a fellow parson's daughter, who so loved the open air, had not been buried at the foot of her beloved moor but lay beneath the floor of the chapel where her Father once preached. My heart beckoned to her deceased spirit as I trampled the earth she so loved, through bracken and heather, all the way up to Top Withens, as featured in her book *Wuthering Heights*. From there I feasted my senses upon the awesome wild and rugged landscape that caused my heart to soar with elation at the beauty and grandeur of this world. Patchwork fields edged in dry stone walling stretched for miles while the longer, wilder grass of the moors danced in the breeze creating numerous shades of green, like the nap of a velvet sheet, as it brushed in opposite directions.

Enriched and captivated by the magnificence of the moors I did feel at home as I removed my shoes and felt the earth's natural energy seep into my being through the soles of my bare feet, but then I suppose thousands of other people feel that way too when nature captures the heart. I'm not sure what I expected to feel on my return to Allerton or what it was I thought I'd find or feel; peace and acceptance probably, but in reality I don't belong here; it was once the village where I lived but it no longer is. When I left, my friends made new friends, life moved on naturally. It was the same in Skipton, when I walked along the high street lined with market stalls and stood on the humpbacked bridge over the canal, nobody recognised me nor I them. Much water has flowed under the bridge since the time that I lived and had been happy here. I've often thought of myself as a Yorkshire lass, and it's true that a part of my roots stem from here through my grandmother, but my accent dissolved and evolved within a short time of leaving. From Yorkshire I will take all the happy memories and picture the smiling faces of those who were my friends and accept all that enhanced my life and helped me to grow. All the heavy baggage and sadness I'll offer to the wind and allow it to dissipate. I leave Yorkshire in love and will visit again sometime to partake of its beauty.

I have wanted to go to India for many years. Timu has been a few times, once with Jim and at others with his family. I've always promised myself that one day I would go but I've always put that day off. Once I embarked upon this book I realised that I had to consider turning the thought into a reality, but in all honesty I was really, really, scared. Scared of what has now become unknown to me, scared of the cultural differences, scared of any emotional reactions I may unleash and scared because my sister-in-law told me a few horror stories on her first return. I put the idea to Rock cautiously,

'I'd really like to go to India darling, how do you feel about us going for a holiday?'

'You have got to be joking', he replied.

'So is that a yes or a no?' I queried.

'It's a no', he asserted, but then I caught him musing and he tentatively asked,

'Will I have to have injections?' And so it was that the seed began to take root and in a short time I was mopping his brow with one hand while he squeezed the fingers of my other tightly as the nurse stuck her needle into his arm. On a cold, dark November morning we were driven, by our son and daughter, to Heathrow airport. They were jolly and light-hearted at the prospect of a day in London to do some Christmas shopping while Rock and I were quiet and filled with apprehension as we swallowed our malaria tablets. They dropped us off outside the terminal and we clung to them desperately, as though we were never going to see them again, we kissed them a thousand times and showered them with words of love and adoration. They in turn hugged us, patted us on the shoulder and with beaming smiles said,

'Go on, you'll have a great time, enjoy yourselves and we'll pick you up in three weeks' time. Bye'.

Feeling alone and dejected we trundled into the terminal building dragging our suitcases behind us. My head hung low and my eyes blindly scoured the floor, so I didn't notice the famous man that I bumped into, even when I apologised and he accepted with a smile. Rock's jaw dropped in awe at the sight of a member of a highly acclaimed band and marvelled at the fact that I hadn't even registered who he was, but I hadn't felt so anxious since the last day I'd spent in school. I passed through all the security checks as though in a daze while trying to convince myself that I was acting completely unreasonably; after all people take these kind of trips every day and my own parents had travelled to India without a return ticket in their travel wallets. I pulled myself together as I boarded the plane and sought out my seat.

I had a pre-booked window seat but was sandwiched between two very assertive fellow passengers. The man in front of me pushed the backrest of his chair as far back as it would go. The little television screen designed for my personal use, attached to the back of it, was so close to my eyes that all I could see was a square blur. The lady behind me was truly one that had been planted for the sole purpose of making the ten hour flight as uncomfortable as it can get. She pushed coats, cardigans and scarves through the narrow space between my chair and the inside of the plane, so that my arm was pushed forward, up and bent in towards me. What she was doing with her knees I have no idea, but they frequently thudded into the small of my back. I like to be next to the window so that I can gaze out at the clouds and read by daylight but the young man next to Rock, in the aisle seat, requested that I pull down the shutter. It was dark and I didn't like it and the man in front, trying to get into a comfortable position, bounced his chair up and down like Disney's Tigger, almost hitting me in the face. Rock slept.

An unusual smell permeated the air, a combination of perfumed oils and British Airways chicken casserole. Lunch was served but there were no chicken dinners left, only the vegetarian option; this suited me fine but Rock, who likes his meat, was not amused. As in-flight meals go it really wasn't bad at all, offering generous portions of saag paneer and curried lentils and with rice and a chapatti on the side. I practised eating with my right hand using no cutlery which wasn't too hard to do considering the position my arm was already forced into. I accepted the complimentary small bottle of red wine but stowed it away in my bag. It would be very welcome upon arrival at the hotel but for now I wanted all my senses strictly intact.

Sometime during the afternoon as we were approaching Moscow, day became night. I had inched my window shutter up during lunch, hoping the chap on the end of our row wouldn't notice. Earth below lit up as a brilliant orangey-red sun sank gracefully into the clouds. It looked like a fire-filled oasis in a grey desert as the sun glowed from beneath us up through the clouds creating a stunning sight, like a vivid red sea transforming as darkness deepened into a furnace of molten glass.

Plunged into the dark of night I relied on the reading light above me when the main lights were dimmed ready for people to take a siesta, and I witnessed my blanket creeping away, being pulled by the passenger behind me. But no matter, the air was warm and I can never sleep on any mode of transport. I was pleased to note that the young man in the aisle seat was slipping into an alcohol-induced doze having seen off four whiskeys and two bottles of wine; he'd been agitated and fidgety since take off. Gradually the peaceful lull of slumber filled the atmosphere and even the bouncer in front of me became still at last, only his snores disturbing the calm.

At eight o'clock in the evening, British time, one-thirty in the morning local time, the plane finally landed with an alarming bump on the runway at Calcutta airport. (I am aware that I'm now obliged to call Calcutta by its new name of Kolkata, but personally I will always think of it in its original form, the capital of Bengal in the northeast of India). A flurry of activity erupted as people scrambled about collecting their belongings together. Overhead lockers were emptied and numerous duty free carrier bags, containing bottles of whiskey, were grasped firmly. Animated, one-sided conversations took place around me as people spoke into mobile phones in a language I could not understand, and the cabin crew took their place in line to bid farewell to what appeared to be an endless stream of people and a powerful stench of accumulated sweat.

Rock and I remained in our seats despite feeling desperate for a breath of non-conditioned air and a stretch of our legs. We looked meaningfully into one another's eyes, each willing the other strength. I was feeling rather less scared now, more overwhelmingly petrified and with all my heart and soul I did not want to leave that plane. It's not that we are unaccustomed to holidays abroad but we're more used to camping in France, lazing in the Canary Islands or enjoying the thrills of Walt's Disney World. Our idea of adventure is a day out at Weston-Super-Mare to gaze at the far distanced sea or a city break enjoying the cultural delights of Rome. Right at that moment I wanted time to rewind and transport me to the comfort of my reclining leather chair in our neutrally decorated lounge to watch Coronation Street on the telly. Instead there we were at a point of no return. We had no option other than to tag onto the queue of people making their way into the airport building.

I've heard it said that you can judge a city by its airport and I wanted, very much, to cry. I transfixed my eyes on the carousel as it wound its way round and round displaying an array of suitcases in a variety of colours. Occasionally somebody would lunge forward in hot pursuit of his or her possessions with an expression of glee at the miracle of reunion. After an hour we had almost given up hope of such a reunion ourselves when a female voice rang out over a loudspeaker. It appeared that, unfortunately, a certain amount of luggage had failed to find its way onto the plane and was sitting waiting patiently back at Heathrow. The voice proceeded to read out a list of names of the people who would not be wearing their own pyjamas that night.

My heart sank and my knees turned to jelly as I mentally ran through the contents of our so carefully packed bags. We couldn't make out any of the names being called but they all sounded like ours. I flew across the unfamiliar airport ready to vent my distress on some poor person with the regrettable job of consoling the inconsolable over their loss. Panic rose within me as I thought about things in the case that I could not possibly live without, even for one night. On reaching the desk, surrounded by equally distraught people, I gave my name to a very beautiful, sari adorned lady who to my immense delight informed me that our luggage should be hitting the carousel any moment now. It had not been left behind and my relief was immeasurable. Sadly, a large number of people were not to share my joy and stood around feeling exhausted and full of despair.

Pulling our wheeled suitcases behind us we headed for the exit and our first breath of warm Indian air. A sea of dark, male faces peered at us from behind a barrier and one of them smiled at us. He waved a sign with our name on it and moved towards us. For a moment we wondered how he knew it was us he was here to meet, until we realised that we were the only white-faced couple in the vicinity. The young, glossy-haired, clean-shaven man of slight build wearing a suit just a tad too big for him, who might have been better advised going to a different optician, proffered his hand in greeting. With much hand shaking he gave his name as Ninty and was pleased to be of assistance to us during our stay.

He led us, authoritatively, through crowds of men offering to carry our bags and a barrage of taxi drivers all pushing and pulling each other in attempts to secure our fare, to a waiting silver Toyota. Banging forcefully on the door Ninty aroused the bemused sleeping driver, who fell at our feet as his door opened, and ushered us into the car. It was three forty-five in the morning as we pulled away from the airport and set off through the city of Calcutta. People thronged the streets, weaving in and out of the busy traffic and wandering the pavements. Bodies lay sleeping as dogs foraged for food in piles of rubbish. Two men guided a herd of goats down the centre of the road as if it were the most natural thing in the world to do, which of course it clearly was here.

The traffic lessened as we turned down back roads away from the central hub of the airport. It began to feel a little eerie in the early morning darkness and Ninty had promptly fallen asleep, leaving Rock and I feeling somewhat vulnerable. Old holy men in Ghandi style dress with long beards meandered along supporting themselves with long walking sticks. Little children sat on the kerbside watching the world go by or playing in the dust. An elderly lady swept the roadside with a witches'-broom-style brush where filth and litter lay in abundance.

We came to a fairly isolated stretch of road where a group of young men stood around a parked truck on one side and a lady, whose age I could not guess, stood with her hands on her hips on the other. We were almost upon them when our car stopped and the driver opened his door. My heart stopped beating and the blood in my veins turned to ice. Horror struck I turned to Rock, whose eyes were like saucers. Ours fears were about to come true: we were going to be robbed, bludgeoned to death, chopped into tiny little pieces and never be seen or heard of again.

We could hear a splashing noise outside the car and, not before time, Ninty woke up. A short discussion took place between the men and then he explained to us that the driver was feeling very sleepy, bless him it was very late, and needed to rinse his face to revive himself. Phew. We exhaled deep sighs of relief and sat back again just a moment too soon. Right ahead of us appeared a huge mob of folk adorned in brightly-coloured clothes and making a lot of noise. They filled the whole road. 'Dear God, now what's going on?' I whispered to Rock who had once again turned a whiter shade of pale. We were terrified and held each other's hand in vice-like grips. I fumbled around the door handle, feeling for a lock but couldn't find one. Our driver slowed down but showed no signs of stopping altogether. This was good. As we drew level with the crowd they simply parted to let us through. 'It's a wedding party', we were informed. 'Oh a wedding', I exuded, 'how lovely'. My nerves were in shreds and I struggled to get my breath but I nearly shot out of my skin when a face pressed up against my window. It was only a pretty young girl taking a curious look at a couple of white people. She smiled and I, somehow, managed to smile back.

With great relief we finally arrived at the *Taj Bengal Hotel* and I was overjoyed at the sheer opulence of the entrance foyer, it was as though I had stepped into an enchanting marble palace. Our suitcases were taken from us and away out of sight the moment we approached the reception desk. We checked in and were shown to our room which, we were delighted to discover, was actually a suite. Our cases arrived and as Rock tipped the man who had brought them my eyes alighted on a bottle of red wine. Oh deep joy. It was a gift from the management and I wanted to throw myself prostate at their feet in gratitude. It had been a long and exhausting day and we were both a little highly strung. After a quick shower we changed into fluffy white hotel dressing gowns and settled ourselves on the enormous bed with its luxuriously thick pillows. For the next hour or so we sipped wine and watched 'Bollywood' films on television and sank into a supremely blissful state of mind.

KOLKATA STREETS

I would like to have stood still for a moment just to stand and stare, as the poem goes, but it proved difficult and inadvisable so I allowed myself to be ushered along with the flow of people heading in the same direction as I now found myself taking. I was completely bewildered and astonished. Of the many scenarios I had played through my mind's eye, none of them had captured the intensity of this city. There was barely a clear space of ground; it was completely consumed by activity. Traders displayed their merchandise along the pavements, people walked, four or five abreast, dogs roamed amongst discarded rubbish and families camped out in huddles. The roads were full to bursting with traffic amongst a sea of bright yellow Ambassador taxis.

I felt a little hand tapping my left arm as a woman shadowed me on my right. The small boy on my left called me Auntie, repeatedly. 'Please Auntie, please Auntie, please Auntie...' He tapped me with one hand while holding his other hand, palm up, towards me. He had an adorable little face with huge brown eyes and an impish grin. The woman to my right was less appealing, indeed rather menacing as she turned her deeply lined, unsmiling face to mine and looked directly into my eyes with a penetrating stare, leaving very little space between our faces. Fortunately she gave up after a while but was soon replaced by a teenage girl. The little boy was delighted with my offering and ran off but, alas, the action enticed five of his friends to come and hound me. Rock was having similar problems: a young mother clutching a runny-nosed baby stuck to his side like glue. 'Milka sir, milka for the baby, milka father...' she persisted constantly as she waved an empty feeding-bottle in front of his face. There was no let-up. As one pleading person or child gave up, another immediately replaced them.

The suffocating heat and relentless tooting of car, bus and truck horns was exhausting. The place was alive with energy and noise. Another young mother clutched my arm and began to chant for money for food for her child. At that point mounting panic rose and threatened to explode in my chest when suddenly, from out of nowhere appeared a vision in my mind of my own young mother walking these very streets being hounded just as I. She was fully composed and in control of herself as she assertively made a gesture with her right arm, drawing it sharply across her front and straight back down by her side exclaiming clearly, 'No'. I imitated her and it worked. Without batting an eyelid or even looking at me as though I had been very rude, the woman begging me fell silent and went in search of her next victim. I felt immediately infused with hope. Having been unable to take in my surroundings as I struggled with a complex series of emotions as to how to deal with so many pleading people, to give or not to give had become a most serious question. I was aware that begging had become a lucrative profession, but when the eyes of a thin and raggedly dressed child or the emaciated face of a mother looks into yours it tears the heart strings. My throat filled with a golf-ball-sized lump and my conscience performed somersaults. I felt swamped with compassion but knew that any offering I proffered to a child would end up in the hands of his or her, for want of a better word, pimp.

We were on the Chowringhee Road in Calcutta, a thoroughfare of the city. Small roads and alleyways ran off it and the depth of anguish Jimmy and Irene must have felt on the day that I, as a two year old tot, ran off became clear to me. This was no place for a child to be lost, the busyness of the road would have been no less then than now. As I peered down one of the alleyways crowded with people I recalled Jim telling me his fears as he lay on his stomach to catch a glimpse of me. If he hadn't found me I would indeed have become one more beggar child suffering at the hands of some entrepreneur of the underworld and would most probably have been groomed into prostitution. The idea curdled my brain and I felt deep gratitude towards my father for his ingenuity in rescuing me and scooping me up into the safety of his arms. It brought the plight of the poor little mites around me much closer to home and my heart went out to them as the familiar phrase came into my mind: 'There, but for the grace of God, go I'.

Rock and I turned into New Market, an indoor market hall off the Chowringhee Road. This had been one of Irene's favourite places to shop and I was eager to see it. It was not dissimilar to many English market places but the selling tactics were far more obtuse. We found it impossible to browse and take a look at the goods for sale. We were hounded with every step we took. Every few yards someone would jump out in front of us and proceed to drape Rock in shirts and me in pashminas. Souvenirs were held before our eyes and perfumed oils under our noses to smell. In the eyes of these people we were rich westerners with money to spend. Indeed we would have loved to spend some money at their stalls, well I certainly would have, but they wouldn't let me look, instead they thrust items towards me. We soon discovered too that to buy one thing was not to satisfy them, 'Why buy one beautiful cotton shirt when you can have three?' they queried. We did get to see the bakery shop, run by a Jewish family, where Irene bought the fresh bread and little pink cakes that Timu so enjoyed, and I felt thrilled indeed to think that I too probably sat in my mother's arms and pointed to something sweet and sticky that took my fancy.

Filled with immense satisfaction at the way our day was turning out we left the market and made our way back out onto the road in search of Babil, the driver of the silver Toyota, who was pleased to take us anywhere we wanted to go. In need of a little respite and in order to regain our equilibrium we asked him to take us to Flury's tea and coffee house on Park Street where we were due to meet up with our guide. During the car journey to Park Street I recalled the advice that Timu had given me regarding eye contact. He'd warned me to keep my eyes averted from others' eyes, as any contact would be seen as a sign of encouragement. In my confusion I had completely disregarded this sound advice out on the streets, which explained the unrelenting pestering. Rock did persist in reminding me but I found it very difficult as I am the sort of person, maybe naive but possibly stupid, who smiles at everyone they pass. I began to realise that it would grant me no peace and also that it was unfair to a seller or beggar who would read my smile as a sign that their family would eat richly that day.

Park Street is the brightly lit place for restaurants, coffee houses and bars. We found Flury's easily with its shocking pink signboard boldly emblazoned above the entrance.

From the outside it looked like any contemporary coffee shop, the style of which may be found in places such as Cheltenham, Chelsea or York. We entered its cool calm gratefully and found a seat by the window allowing us to maintain a view of the outside world but in relative silence. Our ears were ringing with noise. The interior design was rather a surprise: with its brocade seating and the occasional splash of a bright pink accessory, it reminded me more of a German coffee parlour. A huge glass fronted cabinet displayed luscious looking cakes, pastries and confectioneries, the sight of which excited Rock enormously.

Once we had made the decision to come to India we went to a reputable travel company that specialises in finding the perfect trails for travellers. As we had specific places off the beaten track that we wanted to visit we took their advice to hire a guide and a driver. Mala, a gentle Hindu lady who carried herself with graceful deportment arrived and introduced herself as our guide. We discussed an itinerary over a lunch of grilled cheese sandwiches and refreshing fresh lime sodas. Although we had not been in the least bit hungry when we came in, the sight of the cakes, and for me the smell of freshly baked bread, soon awoke our appetites. It was the most delicious toasted sandwich, oozing with melted cheese, that I have ever tasted, and Rock positively drooled over his lemon cake. The whole lunch including drinks and coffees came to the equivalent of under three English pounds. No wonder it had been a favourite haunt of Jimmy's on his visits back to India in later years as it was quiet, clean, luxurious and, to a westerner, cheap. I doubt very much that he and Irene came much to Park Street during the time they lived here as Mala told us that at that time it was a very bohemian area full of restaurants and entertainment. They wouldn't have come for the entertainment and they didn't have enough money to eat out in restaurants.

Tomorrow was to be a 'big' day; a very special day in that Mala and Babil would be taking us to Barrackpore, a suburb of Kolkata, sitting on the other side of the Hooghly River, where we would endeavour to find the house, if indeed it still stood, where Jimmy, Irene, Timu and I had lived. But for the remainder of today Mala suggested a bit of sightseeing. I mentioned the flower market, another place that Irene used to like to go. 'Yes we can go there', she agreed happily, 'and I'll take you to the artisan centre where they make all the statues, garlands and decorations for Hindu festivals. You will find it all very interesting'. We got in the car again and I felt excited about seeing all the colourful flowers and the brightly painted statues. I thought it might be a little gentler than the morning's town walk-about. I was very wrong.

Babil pulled the car up beside a collection of huts at the end of a narrow alleyway. The road was soggy and grey with mud and scattered with barefoot children and dogs. 'Why has he stopped here?' I wondered with growing concern as I watched Mala get out of the front passenger door. I threw Rock an imploring look which he acted upon by asking Mala where we were. 'This is the artisan area', she answered matter-of-factly. 'You cannot be serious', was my only thought as I opened my door and put my foot into something soft, brown and sticky. Thankfully I had favoured trainers in place of flip-flops that day. We followed Mala down the first alley, taking care to step over the overflowing, open drain that was merrily making its stream-like way down the road.

Mala stopped at each little hut where men in *dhotis* were busy making models out of paper, straw and clay. I really tried to listen to her commentary but the further we disappeared into the warren the lighter my head became. Culture shock was in overdrive and I was very afraid, of what precisely I was not sure, simply the difference to all that I have grown accustomed to, I guess. My breathing became rapid and I was sure I was going to pass out. Not something I relished the thought of in this mud mingled with shit covered ground. The insides of the huts were dark, with no electrical lighting, and men squatted on the floor as they worked. The darkness of their skin blended into the darkness of the hut so that all I could see at first glance was the white of their eyes and teeth. Each time she stopped for us to appreciate a model in greater detail I had to quell the urge to scream and encourage her forward. Hungry looking stray dogs roamed around our ankles, and I hadn't had a rabies injection. Everything was turning into a terror stricken-blur and I thought the end would never come. At last I could see light at the end of the tunnel in the form of Babil's smiling face as he stood leaning against the car. The sight brought joy to my jittery heart. With sanctuary within a stone's throw I found I was able to take in what one of the men, via Mala's translation, was telling us. The boldly coloured statue of the four armed, black haired, red lipped goddess Kali, that he was adding the finishing touches to would be recycled after it had been lowered slowly and respectfully into the sacred water of the River Ganges in ceremonial tradition.

 It did seem a dreadful shame to have poured your heart and soul into creating such a glorious and intricate work of art and then have it thrown away. But of course they are not merely thrown away, they are launched as sacred offerings to the gods. Nothing is wasted; the plaster idols will float along the holy waters of the Ganges to the ocean, taking with them all the joys and heartaches of the people of Calcutta.

The models are made out of totally natural materials and will slowly return to the elements from which they were created. After some time, what is left of them, as they drift back to shore will be gathered up and re-used for future ceremonies. We reached a laughing Babil back at the car, where a mother and her three bare-bottomed children lay asleep in the shade beneath it. The day's marvels continued.

By mid-afternoon the fresh lime soda from lunch plus the contents of my water bottle were making urgent requests to leave my body. I whispered my need to Mala, who directed Babil to a Jain temple close by. She guided me across a road, passing by a Hindu shrine, smelling wonderfully of sandalwood, and surrounded by children who charged at me with their little hands outstretched. A public toilet stood in the grounds of the temple, and I went into the Ladies. I was a little taken aback. 'How do I execute this procedure?' I wondered. The latrine I could get the measure of, but the tap coming from the wall about six inches above the floor connected to a hose had me perplexed. Then there was the jug standing next to the hosepipe presenting me with a further challenge. I determined to drink less in the next few days.

The Jain temple was outstandingly beautiful and I couldn't resist taking a closer look. Rock, who had also decided to make use of the public convenience, joined me with a surprised expression on his face and a furrowed brow. The temple shone like a crystal jewel in the sun, a highly decorative, intricately sculpted, multi-steepled building edged in gold. We moved to take a look inside and Mala reminded us to remove our shoes. A gentleman stood guarding a collection of shoes and said he would keep an eye on ours also. The temple's interior walls were covered in tiny mosaics of mirrored tiles and sky-blue ceramics, offering instant cool from the heat of the day.

Jainism has much in common with Hinduism in that they both believe in the notion of cosmology. It is one of the oldest religions, or ways of life, in India and seeks to attain *Moksha* or release from an eternal cycle of life and death through a life of asceticism and in particular a life of non-violence or *Ahimsa*. Living a non-violent lifestyle is taken very seriously, even to the point of dictating a person's choice of job or profession. Farming, for instance, would be considered unacceptable as this could involve the killing of animals; even agricultural work could result in the death of small living creatures during the process of soil turning. Any work that involves aggressive interactions with others, human or animal, is to be avoided. Jains are vegetarians and such is their aversion to harming living creatures that some carry small brushes with them to clear the path as they walk, so as not to crush an insect. Others wear small face masks to prevent them from, inadvertently, swallowing a fly. What they do find to eat I am not entirely sure. They are all responsible for their own actions and the accruing of Karma. Anti-social behaviour such as greed, dishonesty, or aggression will result in an accumulation of Karma and prevent the soul from escaping the consequence and never-ending cycle of rebirth. It's a matter of cause and effect.

Cooled by the temple's shade and revived by its quiet reverence we went to reclaim our shoes, and noting that Mala put some coins into the man's hand Rock followed suit, handing him a one hundred rupee note, about £1.20. He smiled and bowed in profuse thanks. It was only later that we learned an acceptable offering would be in the region of eight to ten rupees.

We headed in the direction of the great Howrah Bridge and my anticipation blossomed. I was very much in need of some earthly grounding. A market full of sweet fragrance, beautifully coloured flowers would calm my frazzled mind and refresh my senses after the hair-raising drive through the city. The car, once again, drew into a crowded area ablaze with bizarre activities. Another wet and splodgy mud-covered road was awash with people and brightly painted trucks. Babil drove ever deeper into the thickening crowd past bright turquoise, fluorescent pink and orange trucks parked frighteningly close to open fires. Women cooked food on the fires as children made mud pies on the road. Men and women sat cross-legged at the side of the road beside mounds of suspicious looking greenery.

Before Mala led us into another warren of dark narrow passageways, lined with crudely built stalls on either side, we went out onto the open space of the *ghat* at the foot of the Howrah Bridge. Poverty and deprivation abounded. Unkempt bodies with matted hair lay around on the stone floor and others wandered listlessly wrapped in filthy rags. Flea-ridden dogs ran around threateningly while men bathed in the holy waters. Some sat on the steps leading down to the water's edge gazing, reverently, out across the river; a group of ladies scrabbled amongst the pile of rubbish heaped on the river bank. It was a deeply humbling sight. An air of deep spirituality filled the space and I felt that maybe I shouldn't be standing watching as souls performed their religious bathing rituals. Something about the light above the water seemed surreal to me and the dark-skinned silhouettes against it formed a captivating, heart-stirring sight and one that I was reluctant to leave.

Inside the market, straw and flower cuttings absorbed the mud on the floor where men and boys sat stringing bright orange marigold petal heads and creamy white jasmine flowers into long garlands. Large open sacks displayed the end products for sale while the stalls were laden with posies, bunches and little basket arrangements of flowers, many with a small candle as the centre piece. My initial distress on arrival, at the thought of weaving my way precariously through the closely packed rows of stallholders, began to dissipate. Agreed, this was not what I had expected, and I had felt a measure of dismay when I realised that I was not about to float through a delightfully scented flower fair. But the colours were radiant and the smell, once my olfactory sense got beyond the earthy rawness of mud, was intoxicating. The dark faces of so many men packed into confined spaces no longer alarmed me. They were simply weary chaps, working every hour under the sun and beyond, in an attempt to put food in their bellies. I resisted the urge to smile at them but looked admiringly at their handiwork.

At the far end of the market we climbed some steps, taking care to allow right of way to *coolies*, those carrying enormous bundles on their heads, and found ourselves on the impressive *Rabindra Setu,* more popularly known as the Howrah Bridge that provides a link across the River Hooghly between Howrah and Calcutta. The bridge had been re-christened as *Rabindra Setu* during 1965 in honour of Rabindranath Tagore, a Nobel Prize winner for literature and a great living institution to his fellow Bengalis. A hugely gifted man who was once known as the voice of India's spiritual heritage across the globe, he was a poet and author and even put his own music to his own songs. Only a bridge as magnificent as this could be worthy of his name in his native land. The cantilevered construction is one of the busiest bridges in the world, carrying the weight of approximately one hundred and fifty thousand vehicles, around two million pedestrians as well a few thousand cattle across its eight traffic lanes and two walkways daily. This gateway to Calcutta is the perfect standpoint for the glorious view of the River Hooghly and the vast ants' nest that is the city of Calcutta. The bridge, crossing holy water, is so revered that the law prohibits photography from it or of it, though many seem to have disregarded this rule as numerous pictures are in evidence.

Standing on the bridge, raised above the crowds and grime, with the calming flow of sacred water beneath us we revelled in a welcome feeling of space and tranquillity. With the sun on our faces and the wind ruffling our hair we were able to fully appreciate the beauty and sparkle of the colourful inhabitants of this city of such great contrasts. We feasted our eyes and drank in the atmosphere for many precious moments. I got a warm and comforting feeling as I wondered if Jimmy and Irene had stood in this same spot and gazed at a similar view some years ago. Had they felt as overwhelmed as I when they arrived as a young and fresh, newly married couple, not for a three week long holiday but to face the challenge of a completely new life? I shuddered at the thought and wondered how they had coped with the adjustments, having been reared in a small coastal village where everyone knew everyone else.

I felt a strange sensation behind me and turned to find a small man with long white hair and a beard, dressed in a long white collarless shirt and no shoes on his feet, taking a close look at me. His wrinkled skin was drawn tightly across his cheekbones and his lips were pursed as he examined me through large, round, puzzled brown eyes. He studied me from varying angles, taking a step to the right then left, cocking his head from side to side like a questioning spaniel. There was nothing threatening or suggestive about his manner, I was simply an object of his curiosity. Others too turned to look as they passed by the pale *Memsahib* in her bland, colourless clothes.

At the other end of the bridge stood Howrah railway station from where we, as a family, had departed to and arrived from many a destination around this country. Mala and Babil were eager to take us onto the main platform. Rock and I watched in fascination as a train pulled in bearing passengers who hung onto the outside. Travelling in this style, in India, is widely known and often depicted on television so it should not have come as a surprise to us, but to watch it happen in real life is truly astonishing. By the time the train had drawn to a full stop only those travelling inside were left to alight, the hangers on had jumped and were well on their way. Passengers awaiting their train sat cross-legged on the floor picnicking or drinking hot, sweet, milky tea bought from a vendor just outside the station, or lay stretched out asleep. One remarkably handsome man with sculptured features, captivating bright, almond-shaped eyes and chin length, thick, glossy black hair that would be the envy of any film star, casually jumped down onto the track. In one slick movement he squatted down low and did a shit before jumping back onto the platform and brushing down his worn cotton *dhoti*. Nobody appeared to protest but one or two, including myself, discreetly put a hand to their nose. Hello India.

BLOW HORN PLEASE!

This day was one that I never really, in my heart of hearts, expected to experience. I found myself standing face to face with a little man from Sikkim, whose round shaped face peeked out from beneath a grey woollen hat as he sat on a low stool and smiled at me. He sat on the veranda, the very same veranda that overlooks the River Hooghly where once my tiny bare feet danced and skipped. The man, who looked like a cute little gnome, smiled widely and spoke to Mala, our guide. Mala turned to me and translated, 'He knew you would come one day. His name is Tipi Guru, and he met your father and your brother when they came here some years ago. Your brother put two baskets of flowers, each with a lit candle in the centre, into the river in memory of your twin brothers'. I knew this to be true. 'Your Dad told this man that one day you would come also. Tipi is pleased that you are here'.

The comment had startled me. How did Jim know that I would feel compelled to come here, that something would draw me to re-visit this house? Yes it's true that I've always said I would one day, but I did not honestly believe that I would. Because I've been so tightly bound by my personal comfort zones and monotonous routines of everyday life I never realised what joys may be waiting beyond my self-inflicted barriers. Perhaps Jim knew or simply hoped that I would someday break free and rise to the challenge that called me.

I'd got out of bed earlier than usual that morning because I was excited about going to Barrackpore. I sat by the window of our hotel room sipping a cup of hot black tea; the road outside was quiet for Calcutta but then it was only five forty-five. To my amazement, out of a ditch at the far side of the main road appeared a man. He stepped onto the pavement and shook himself about a bit then stuck his head under a stand pipe and brushed back his wet hair with his hands before heading off along the road. Within a few minutes he returned with a stack of baskets on his head, laid them out on the ground before him and sat cross-legged behind them to await his first customers. Other people began to climb out of the ditch too: men, women and children; they all swilled their faces under the stand pipe before setting off to the business of the day. Within moments the road was a hive of activity, with parents walking their children to school alongside businessmen and women who clutched briefcases and talked into mobile phones. Women swept the roadside and boys pulled carts, laden with merchandise I assumed they were hoping to sell, artfully through the heavy traffic. It was such an incredibly conflicting sight. Above the ditch, where many homeless people obviously lived by night, stood a massive billboard advertising the sale of luxury apartments only a short distance away. I looked around our beautiful luxury suite and wondered quite what exactly was going on?

After breakfast Rock and I went downstairs to the cool lobby of the hotel where Mala sat graciously waiting to greet us with her engaging smile. Babil brought the silver Toyota to the entrance doors and we climbed in to begin our day's adventure. We drove through the city at an alarming speed considering the amount of traffic on the roads which, incidentally, changes the direction of its one-way system twice a day in an attempt to reduce congestion. We crossed the great Howrah Bridge and entered the more rural suburbs of Calcutta and I had to stop myself from bouncing up and down in my seat with excitement, lest I distract Babil, when we passed a sign informing us we were entering Titigarh. It was a rustic area indeed, a shanty town of tents where many people sat or lay around on the dusty ground, living in what appeared to me appalling conditions of poverty. The thought of my Mum and Dad coming to live and work here, fresh and surely a little naive as to the extent of suffering and poverty that they would encounter, jolted me. For the first time the depth of their love and compassion for other people really hit me. I thought of my mother as a new bride wandering these streets that even now showed little regard for health and safety, as barrels of highly inflammable liquids stood around or were being transported on the back of open trucks. Suddenly, as though it was really happening before my eyes, I caught a vision of my Mum weaving her way amongst the many rickshaws, goats, stray dogs and cattle. She wore a bright pink silk sari that swished as she walked; she smiled and acknowledged people with a friendly touch.

The journey took over an hour by car and the full stretch of our route was active with energy. The roadsides were full to bursting with inhabitants and stall sellers displaying their wares, or piles of fruit and vegetables swarming with flies. Horns never ceased to blow as drivers tooted rather than indicated. Trucks and buses had 'Blow horn please', emblazoned across the backs of their vehicles in a request to let other drivers know they were approaching or to allow them to filter into the stream of fast moving traffic. It was noisy and exhilarating. Children in school uniforms rode in rickshaws with a cage around the carriage to safeguard them, but the poorer children walked; one young boy 'walked' on his hands and bottom as he had no legs.

We were away from the city here and Rock and I, in the back of the car, were of great interest to people sitting on top or hanging from the sides of buses. They craned their necks to take a closer look at the colour, or lack of it, of our skin. Whenever we slowed down, faces pressed up against our windows to view the strange creatures within; it was a little startling and unnerving at times but we soon learnt they meant us no harm. Barrackpore was strikingly different. It welcomed us with a large road sign standing, like a banner, above the wider, clearer road. Here was a more peaceful locality where students ambled along carrying their books. My heart was in my mouth as we entered and passed barracks and a sign to an officers' mess. A most strange sensation began to creep through me and my ears turned deaf to my surroundings. I felt a hammering in my chest. I left here before I was five years old and yet, somehow, forty years later I knew where I was as we followed the signpost to Riverside Road. We came to a college and just to its left, set back behind some large old trees I saw the house, my old house, and I recognised it at once. Babil parked the car by the large pond that Timu and I were warned not to go too near, not only through fear of us drowning but also because snakes slithered in the long grass at its edge. As I peered into the water an enormous black fish swam beneath its surface.

The once white-painted bungalow with its green wooden shutters was in sad disrepair as the original bricks of the grand portico were crumbling. But it was still very beautiful in my sight. We walked from the front of the building around the right-hand side and saw the sun glinting on the River Hooghly. It was there at the back of the house that Tipi Guru sat on his little stool, protecting his domain. He told us that the government paid him to look after the house but Mala explained to us that this could not really be so. Clearly he was just one of four families who squatted there. Tipi pointed to an unsightly lump of cement that he'd slapped into a crack in the wall and wedged with a stick of wood and told us that if he had not taken care of the maintenance the house would have fallen down long ago.

Tipi beckoned his wife from inside the bungalow and she appeared on the veranda carrying a tray with four silver metal cups containing water for us to drink. Rock and I looked at one another aghast at the prospect of drinking on-tap dysentery but fortunately Mala, used to such situations, dealt with it efficiently causing no offence. I drifted into my own little world and found myself peering in through the open doorway at what used to be our living-room. Even the tiles on the floor, now chipped and scruffy, were the same. Tipi must have noticed my distraction and kindly invited me to enter and take a look around the portion of the bungalow that he lived in. I walked into the room and through a doorway saw the bedroom that my parents had once slept in. Dormant memories sprang into life and flooded my mind. In our day there were two kitchens, one in which Ram Smudge cooked his culinary delights and the second one, which Jim had set up for Irene, was where she baked pies and familiar English dishes from home. I could almost smell them baking.

Outside, I wandered off for a moment's solitude and walked down the garden towards the river. Over the years the river has swallowed about half the length of the original garden where our tomatoes and vegetables grew in abundance. A team of men worked at the broken banks, building a wall of protection. They watched me curiously as I stood in reflection with tears of joy dripping onto my cheeks. I had never expected to remember this house and had worried that I wouldn't be able to distinguish it from others, but I could even remember the house close by where my Indian aunties lived and from where I left a trail of paratha crumbs in my wake. I turned to face the back of the bungalow and jumped as a pair of eyes peeked out at me from under a pile of dirty blankets lying on a makeshift bed. I hadn't noticed the man sleeping on the veranda until he scowled at me in confusion before Tipi explained to him who we were and what was going on, and then he smiled.

When the time came to move on I was loath to leave, but the house was no longer mine and I'd seen all there was to see and swum in an ocean of rekindled memories that are mine to hold for as long as I need them. I had found something precious there that formed a missing link and filled an empty space in the jigsaw of my life. I was beginning to understand why I had never fitted snugly into the patterns of the societies and communities of my later years. My formative years, whether I comprehended them or not, had been spent here in this beautiful village, just a small part of this wondrous country, a country enriched with impulse, spontaneity and a certain sense of acceptance. I felt the love that had been showered upon me by friends and neighbours and something sparked into life deep within me as I accepted that for a time, even though the colour of my skin differed from those around me, I had belonged there. Making that journey had been the right and valuable thing for me to do. As I touched the earth of the garden and the bricks and mortar of the house I felt a sense of fulfilment, both physically and emotionally. My heart exploded with love and gratitude for the experiences my parents have given me. In a moment's revelation I recognised that I have not fully appreciated or used wisely all that their love and guidance has offered me. The way in which they lived their lives with love and compassion helped to dissolve barriers of colour and race. Perhaps I have not previously fully acknowledged just how much of a blessing that is to the world.

I watched my husband as he stood talking to Mala a short distance away, and my heart soared with love for him too. The man who tore through his own comfort zone in order to accompany me on my personal journey did it primarily and unselfishly for me. He is indeed my rock and I feel honoured and proud to be his wife and the recipient of his wonderful love. I squeezed his hand in a gesture of thanks as we sat in the back of the car and drove away from the bungalow, watching it slowly disappear from our view. I caught another image of my young mother in her pink sari as she walked along the road carrying me in her arms. Timu walked by her side dressed in a white shirt and red shorts with a red tie around his collar and black polished shoes that contrasted sharply with his brilliant white socks. We were on our way to school where Mum taught the local children as I sat on the floor by her desk scribbling on pieces of paper, pretending to write. Two Indian ladies stopped to greet her and as one of them said something to her my mother threw back her head and laughed, oh how she laughed, with a twinkle in her eyes.

I saw a white building ahead of us and my hand flew to my mouth as I remembered it to be the Wesleyan chapel that we'd gone to on Sundays and where my Dad had preached. I asked Babil to stop the car so that I could take a closer look, and as we all walked around the building we came across the caretaker who lived in a tiny hut in the grounds. He kindly unlocked the door and allowed us to go inside. Again it was as though I had stepped back in time for there, in my imagination, stood my father speaking animatedly to a congregation who sat cross-legged on the floor, with sunshine pouring in through the windows and lighting up their faces. Mala asked the caretaker if he had any records or ledgers from days gone by stored anywhere. He didn't, but he suggested that we go a little further down the road to St. Bartholomew's church which would, in Jim's time, have been the Anglican place of worship but where he, nevertheless, led a service once a month. This church, along with the Wesleyan chapel are now part of the Church of North India, as amalgamation did finally take place with all Christian denominations merging into one.

We were warmly welcomed at St. Bartholomew's by a charming English-speaking man who had been clerk there for the past thirty-eight years. The reason for our visit delighted him and he put himself to a great deal of trouble to locate the ledgers of the mid 1950s to mid 1960s. I was deeply enthralled by the heavy old record books that contained page upon page of my Dad's bold, flowing signature written in ink, verifying the marriages, births, baptisms and burials that he had presided over. I recognised other names on registers and as I read them out aloud I smiled, recalling the Bishop who had stayed with us in Allerton for a time when he was over in England on matters of the Church. 'You know this man?' asked the clerk, and when I said that I did, he immediately picked up his telephone and dialled a number. After a brief introduction the Bishop's rich laughter filled the room as the telephone was handed to me. We enjoyed a long conversation with much reminiscence, and all the while Mala's expression was one of incredulity, as apparently the Bishop I speak of became a prominent and well known, highly regarded figure and sociologist in Calcutta. We later enjoyed a conversation about the Church of North India with the Bishop of Barrackpore who was called in by our host the clerk to meet us, and Rock and I felt a little like visiting celebrities. It was a truly wonderful experience that gave me a deeper insight into the life and work of my parents and for a fleeting moment brought them back to life.

I was overjoyed and bubbling with happiness as we took our leave of Barrackpore and joined the throng of horn blowers on the main road back to Calcutta. Suddenly all the cars in our stream took a sharp swerve to the right and a few grazed paint in mild collision with each other. But not ours, as Babil was on the ball. On our left stood the reason for the diversion, tethered to a pole, drinking water from a bucket. Many Hindus will go to any length to avoid harming the life of a sacred cow and clearly in this incident the risk of a traffic pile-up was preferable. However, I wasn't sure that the poor little fellow who was filling a pot-hole in the middle of the road with hot tarmac felt the same way as he jumped onto the bonnet of a swerving car in a swift act of self-preservation.

PEACEFUL CONTENTMENT

At the end of our fascinating week in Calcutta we flew south to spend a few days in Cochin before driving to Alleppey to board our floating hotel. We spent twenty-four hours on a boat made from wood and coir roping and were escorted by three local men through the backwaters. It was a soothing and peaceful trip, taking in the beauty of palm trees that shade the small islands and their inhabitants. The waters were adorned with an aggressive growth of water hyacinths that bloom beautifully, but sadly threaten the ecology of the canals. Rock and I were accompanied by delightful birds that entertained us with their swooping antics and serenaded us with their song. Women smiled and waved to us graciously as they went about their daily chores and washed their laundry in the waters before hanging it out to dry beneath the hot sun. I wondered if they objected to us gently sailing by their dwellings and gawping at them. A small boy squealed in delight as his father soaped his body then dunked him in the waters to rinse him clean. Children dressed in red and white school uniforms walked in crocodile lines to a ferry waiting to take them to school in the village. We saw a lifestyle far removed from our own, and yet it still rang with the familiarity of routine.

Our crew of three were made up of a captain who steered the boat, a host who served our food and drinks and a cook. The captain was missing a little toe on his left foot and I cringed as our host explained how the toe had got caught up in an anchor's rope and been pulled off. We didn't get to see much of the cook as he was kept busy preparing an endless supply of courses that our host proudly brought to our table, set on the front deck of the boat beneath the shade of a thatched canopy. The food was delicious and consisted mainly of fresh fish caught in the backwaters. Even here, in what appeared to be the middle of nowhere, salesmen plied their trade. As I relaxed on deck I was startled when a pair of eyes peered over the side of our boat. A man with a toothy grin and bright sparkling eyes held up a wriggling fish for my inspection and offered it to me for a very good price. I knew not what to do with the fish for we already had a bountiful supply of food but I suggested he show our cook anyway.

I began to feel extremely delicate after our evening meal and put it down to the unaccustomed richness of the dishes, added to the effect of the swaying boat. It was only when we anchored for the night and I began to pay frequent trips to the bio-loo housed in our sleeping quarters that I realised why I may be suffering. Rock had already suffered from a few cases of dodgy belly in Calcutta and moaned that I must have internal immunity left over from childhood, for which I was very grateful. But as we 'parked' after sunset within short distance of other boats, all similar to ours, we were able to see their crews relaxing. The men called to one another from boat to boat as they bathed, cleaned their teeth, relieved themselves and washed up the crockery, cutlery and glasses that our food and drinks had been served on in the canal. The pots and pans they dangled on ropes to soak for a while.

I was a little stunned and thought maybe I'd pass on breakfast, but I was also quite thrilled because, after all, we had come to see the real India. I do have to admit that Rock and I were not terribly brave during the long night. The setting was eerie and dark. Unfamiliar sounds startled us and we frequently peeked out of the small windows to see the shape of canoes beneath human silhouettes set against the night sky as they floated by. The occasional light flickered and made us jump, but it was the water rats that had us tangled up inside the mosquito net as we furiously wound up our torch to spot them before they spotted us. Around the early hours, as I lay exhausted from lack of sleep, the call from the mosque lulled me into a peaceful stillness and I pulled back the curtain to watch the sunrise.

I was quite relieved when our boat finally docked in the morning, for the food we had been served was taking a fast track through my body. I grew increasingly concerned when Manoj, our new driver, introduced himself and happily informed us that it would take approximately four hours by road to reach our next destination. An interesting afternoon ensued as we leisurely drove through Indian villages and captured a sense of their culture, a delight we would have missed had we flown by aeroplane. The drive was at times hair-raising and bumpy, very, very bumpy and all the while the contents of our stomachs were fighting to find the quickest exit. We tried to concentrate hard and take in the many colourful goings on taking place around us, but with no motorway service stations en route it was a bit of a struggle. The best and most welcome comfort stop of the day came in the form of a Hindu temple. Manoj took us to a beautiful and elaborately decorated temple full of intricately carved statues to have a look around and stretch our legs. It was an enthralling sight to behold and I found myself smiling at a resplendent image of Ganesha, the elephant god worshipped as a bringer of good luck, remover of difficulties and obstacles and a god of wisdom and patron of learning. As we left the temple we were encouraged to dip our fingers in a paste of crushed sandalwood mixed with water and put a dab of it in the centre of our foreheads. We were instantly cooled against the heat of the day and much to our relief the sickening bubbling of our tummies quelled.

We spent ten blissfully relaxing days in Kovalam swimming in a warm infinity pool that overlooked a palm-fringed beach edging the Arabian Sea. We walked along golden sands and bought silk kaftans from sellers who offered them, 'as cheap as chips', or 'buy one get one free'. At the end of tranquil days, perfumed by the sweet fragrance of jasmine flowers, we sampled culinary wonders at an open restaurant tucked into a tropical garden. The waiters were charming and served us with grace, but no matter what we ordered to eat they raised their eyebrows and asked, 'May I suggest...?' And so it was that we often ended up with a dish we would never have thought of trying and in some cases wished we had not. Our suitcases were a few pounds heavier and our bodies a few pounds lighter as we flew from Kerala, the land of coconuts, to Mumbai for the last leg of our trip.

Shortly after takeoff on our homebound flight out of Mumbai, hysteria rose in my chest. The captain of the aeroplane's voice announced, 'Ladies and Gentlemen, it is with regret that I have to inform you that we are in trouble'. In a high state of anxiety I frantically tried to remember all the safety procedures as given to us by the cabin crew before takeoff. The thundering blood rush pumping through my brain prevented me from hearing the rest of the announcement as I scrambled to push my head to my knees and clutch the back of my neck in the brace position. Rock laughed and pulled me back into my seat, explaining that the captain had gone on to say, 'We have lost our radio connection and no longer have access to the cricket results'.

*

I left India with regret and a myriad of thoughts to occupy my mind. I realised as I walked into my kitchen back home that the best part of being home is the luxury, one I have previously taken for granted, of turning on the tap to produce a clean supply of drinking water. Over the weeks spent in a country that I have once again come to love, my life has been transformed. Not only have my boundaries been stretched but my heart has been set free. By 'meeting' my parents again and by 'seeing' my mother so full of beauty and life, it is as though she has been lifted from the limbo between life and death. I have allowed the restrictive and bulky collar around her neck to slip loose and fall onto the pillow. She is free to shake her head and run her hands through her hair. I can see her laughing as she rises up from the hospital bed and walks away. My memories of her in immense pain and discomfort have transformed into living images of the woman she has really been in life. I have witnessed what she was up against when she lived in India and I can understand how difficult life must have been for her at times. I now feel free to let her go in love to death and free to let her live again in my heart. The pain of loss is beginning to ease and the heavy weight of guilt is lifting, because I know how distressed she would be if she knew how I carried it around. She is resurrected and I feel more peacefully content.

Jimmy had the gift of the gab and could tell a good tale; could he have sold coals to Calcutta? Yes I believe he really could, but I also know that he would never have even tried because his integrity would not have entertained such a fiddle.

I have never really considered my Dad to be an evangelist. I saw him more as a man of deep faith who centred on his faith to go out and work towards peace and justice and the overriding of evil in the world from wherever he found himself placed. Whether he was happy to be in each given situation or not, he strove to find contentment within himself so that he could concentrate fully on the needs of the particular society or environment in which he stood. In this light I have wondered in more recent years how he reconciled his missionary work, going into a foreign land with an aim to convert people of other faiths to Christianity, with all I know of his passion for harmony between faiths and denominations.

My dad was a great scribbler. He never went anywhere without a pencil and a piece of paper. He jotted notes on the back of envelopes, receipts, in fact anything that came to hand and I have inherited that peculiar habit from him. When the time came to clear out my parents' home after their deaths I found orderly sermon notes, all neatly filed, and bundles of scribbles stashed into the drawer beside his chair in the lounge. I discovered a worn piece of paper entitled, 'The Right to Believe'. Jim's familiar handwriting read:

'As a missionary I went to convert, following the great command, "Go...." I learnt a lot about myself and other people's convictions and beliefs. I began to take a completely different approach, especially in Southall. Aggressive evangelism is not the way. My interest and study is not so much Sikhism, Islam,

Hinduism – but the Sikh people, the Muslim people, the Hindu people. Living in another country in an alien situation, what are their needs? Language, faith, education? The pressure of Western secular society. Buildings for worship – to express their faiths – does, should the Church help? The Holy Spirit converts, not us. We are called to witness by our lives, simplicity, humility, sharing – dialogue. We need to articulate the gospel in ways other faiths can understand. We need to check our technical Christian jargon and what it means'.

So there I had my answer. A young, intense and enthusiastic Jimmy went to India with the intention of filling his church with new members to praise the Lord and shout Hallelujah. He soon discovered his own naivety and vulnerability when living in another land, yet he adapted and integrated and grew in self and circumstantial awareness. In Southall he had much to offer because of his experiences. When trouble struck the community the people of all faiths came together as people of God. When Jim was criticised for his stance he was accused of putting Christianity at risk. His response was, *'Mission is risk. To read and study other major faiths at a distance is safe perhaps, to worship and share with them risks drawing power'.*

*

As I took my leave of County Durham I felt as though I carried a part of my family's history with me. I had gained much insight into my roots and felt fulfilled and satisfied as I drove cross-county to join the motorway that would lead me back to Worcestershire and my family. I played a favourite CD that never fails to bring me pleasure, yet this time it held greater significance. I turned up the volume and sang along, in not too graceful accompaniment, with the men of Wales as their rich voices told the joys of the *Land of my fathers*, or in my case the land of my great grandfather. Between the tuneful strains of the Welsh male voice choir and the worn brick that sat on the passenger seat next to me, I had reminders of my roots.

I met up with my cousin Keith and his wife Carole, while in the North East of England, and they took me to Kelloe to show me the village where our joint grandfather, my dad's father, had been born. We stood outside Saint Helen's Church and guessed we were somewhere near the terrace that bore the same name. Carole spotted a man who with the aid of a walking stick was heading off along a footpath. She called to him and he offered to lead us through a field and show us where the remains of Saint Helen's Terrace still lay. We were soon joined by two of the gentleman's friends who told us that the foundations we walked upon were the original stone floors of the cottages. We were able to distinguish each individual plot and counted them up to house number eight where Jim Parkinson senior had been born, the seventh child of eight, and touched the stone that once grazed the knees of our grandfather in his infancy. It was one of those touching moments that bridges the present with the past.

Our three gentlemen friends pointed out where the pit's spoil heap, now amass with the growth of young trees, once stood within close view of the house, and described how the pit had stood at its far side. It was the pit where our great-grandfather had laboured. To the edge of the stone foundations lay a line of bricks forming the outline of the terrace. Keith and I each bent down to touch a brick, and with a knowing look at one another managed to wriggle a couple loose and hold them lovingly, mud and all, close to our chests. As we dusted them clean we bade farewell to our helpful and friendly companions as they disappeared across the road into a tree lined tunnel, tipping their flat caps and waving their sticks in salute. We felt as though we had just played a scene in *The last of the summer wine*.

Having made a connection with my roots as I drove from Durham through Yorkshire, I felt pleased that my passion for Welsh male voice choirs, a curiosity that has bewildered Rock for years, combines to tie the three counties together. Maybe sometime I will delve further into my family's history and discover where our DNA originates from, possibly Africa, just going to prove that we in this world really are all in it together. Although much north eastern blood courses through my veins, it flows with the love and spirit of India that has played a large part in moulding me, a part that I honour and will no more take for granted.

I am not entirely sure why I have never grown to connect with Worcestershire and come to think of it as home, even though it has been for most of my married life. Rock was born here, as were his parents, and it is where his family roots through many generations belong. He and I met while on a weekend trip to Paris, neutral ground for us both, and after we married I left Southall to come and live in his home town. Being used to moving around I soon settled in and made new friends, but this time I found it a little more complicated. Because Rock had grown up here his history was all around me and I felt oddly alone surrounded by people who knew things about him that I didn't. It felt strange to me because in all my past relocations my family and I were equals in our newness and could share the unfamiliarity. Even when my parents retired and moved here to be near us, the sense of home still evaded me and I don't know why, perhaps it was simply a lack of personal history.

Perhaps a part of me refused to co-operate fully because I had had to leave all that was familiar to me. From this experience I have gained empathy towards people who, for reasons particular to them, have moved to Great Britain from their native homeland and struggle to integrate fully into British or Western society. For those who have been exiled and torn from their roots it must be traumatic in the extreme. Integration in all its guises demands great depth of tolerance and acceptance from all sides and requires dialogue steeped in respect and sensitivity. I find the word *Namaste* to be particularly beautiful in its intent, 'I bow to you', or 'the light within me honours the light within you'. I see its message as recognition of our differences, no matter how great or small, yet offering a meeting place that is based on mutual respect in a spirit of love and compassion.

My quest has strengthened me and I have become my own person at last. I have turned around and can see the spectacular beauty that I have previously closed my eyes to in this lush county of Worcestershire. Obstinacy did not become me, it simply held me back. If home is where the heart is then I am in the right place. I am by nature a quiet person who prefers not to be in the spotlight, unlike Rock who holds a crowd well as he sings and I am deeply proud of him. I have learnt to embrace my quiet nature and need for solitude and in accepting these things about myself, rather than fighting against them, I have become more accepting of others. Rock and I are an odd couple I guess; he loves to hear the sounds of music at all times, and believe me our children will testify to the diversity of his tastes, while I like the sound of silence unless I am driving. He thrives on live concerts and I prefer to read a book, and yet we blend beautifully together in harmony, I tell him what to do and he obeys; no, not at all, of course I'm joking, a bit. Seriously though, we have found that we have mutual respect and understanding for one another's needs and interests. We've had our troubles of course, yet perhaps because of the times in which we have almost chosen to go in opposite directions the depth of our friendship, which is more precious than anything money can buy, draws us ever closer together. In each other we have found a shared space to 'be'.

Yesterday was Saint Valentine's. I bathed in exotic oils from India and dressed carefully. Rock took the stairs two at a time and burst into our bedroom, his face aglow with delight. 'Come and look', he beckoned, 'come and see the flowers'. Bursting with excitement and anticipation I ran my hands through my hair and followed him downstairs. I entered the kitchen in his wake and ran my eyes around the room in search of the bouquet of red roses. I found none, so followed him into the conservatory where he gently took my hand and said, 'Look, look'. His eyes were moist with wonder and emotion as I traced their gaze to the jasmine plant that I had bought him for his last birthday. Overnight the rich green foliage had given birth to a perfect star-like white flower and many tightly curled buds that promised to bloom. I watched Rock smell the sweet fragrance and saw the strong man that is my husband melt in sheer joy at such beauty. That tiny little flower had captured his heart and I had never loved him so much.

*

Now, as I enter my study I greet the smiling faces of Jim and Irene Parkinson, and feel deeply proud that they were my parents. As I dust the frame which holds their photograph I pay honour to them for all they have been to me and for all they have been to the many other people that they walked with on their journey. I turn around in my hand the ornamental pit boots that stand on my desk and think of all the miners who have suffered and laboured under harsh conditions, and of all the bellies that screamed out for food during the long, traumatic strikes. I pay tribute to them all. Praem Chand, the leper, though no longer on this earth still enters my dreams. I see his smile and his shining blue eyes that once held me captive; as a child I saw only his beauty and his love, both will remain with me always. Then I pick up the grey fluffy elephant that goes by the name of Squidgy, and I laugh as I bring to mind the memories it holds in the stuffing of its heart.

I have fullness of love in family and friends past, present and yet still to meet across the globe in the future I hope, and I feel thankful. In God I feel free to love and be loved in return. As I conclude this journey I realise that it will continue for as long as I have air to breathe. I thank my parents for their nurture and for presenting me with a life rich in mystery that insists on my ever increasing quest for love and knowledge. I will not cease to question, explore, prune and weed as my journey moves forward. This search has freed me from limitations of fear that once held me back. I do not know what is around the next corner or what I face when I die, but my most heartfelt wish is that in life and in death we all find a way to recognise each other by love.

Namaste